If I Should
DIE
Before I
LIVE

Meditations for Seniors

by

Richard Renwick Smyth

LOGOS BOOKS, ASHEVILLE, NORTH CAROLINA

www.ChironPublications.com

Logos Books is a book imprint of Chiron Publications
Interior and cover design by Daliborka Mijailović
Printed primarily in the United States of America

All scripture quotations are from the New Revised Standard Version Bible unless otherwise indicated, copyright 1989, Division of Christian Education of the National Council of the Churches of Christ in the United States of America. Used by permission. All rights reserved.
Scripture quotations marked Peterson are taken from THE MESSAGE, copyright © 1993, 1994, 1995, 1996, 2000, 2001, 2002 by Eugene H. Peterson. Used by permission of NavPress. All rights reserved. Represented by Tyndale House Publishers, Inc.

ISBN 978-1-63051-473-0 paperback
ISBN 978-1-63051-474-7 hardcover
ISBN 978-1-63051-475-4 electronic
ISBN 978-1-63051-476-1 Limited Edition

Library of Congress Cataloging-in-Publication Data

Names: Smyth, Richard Renwick, author.
Title: If I should die before I live : meditations for seniors / Richard Renwick Smyth.
Description: Asheville : Chiron Publications, 2017. | Includes bibliographical references and index.
Identifiers: LCCN 2017050412| ISBN 9781630514730 (pbk. : alk. paper) | ISBN 9781630514747 (hardcover : alk. paper)
Subjects: LCSH: Older people--Religious life--Meditations. | Aging--Religious aspects--Christianity--Meditations. | Death--Religious aspects--Christianity--Meditations.
Classification: LCC BV4435 .S69 2017 | DDC 242/.65--dc23
LC record available at https://lccn.loc.gov/2017050412

Dedication

To Sylvia, my wife,

who shares the exploration

Praise for *If I Should Die Before I Live*

"*If I Should Die Before I Live* could well become a devotional classic. I deeply appreciate the inspiration it has bought."

-Rev. Charles A. Sayre, Ph.D., former pastor, Haddonfield (NJ) United Methodist Church

"The meditations, each taking about ten minutes to read, will become an inspiration for people of all ages and a helpful conversation starter for small groups. I encourage you to read a series of meditations written by one with a pastor's heart, a scholar's mind, a disciple's devotion and an apostle's abiding commitment to share the good news that inspires us in life, in death and in life beyond death."

-Rev. Gregg A. Mast, Ph.D., President Emeritus, New Brunswick Theological Seminary

Table of Contents

Exploration II

Exploration III

Author's Preface

James Michener's *The Source* traces cultural origins in the east Mediterranean basin. He sets the novel at an archaeological site. Ancient relics at the deepest excavation indicate beginnings of human social life. Michener introduces: Ur (a hunter of food), his wife, and daughter. A young man wanders into their world, their life. The youth (a grower of food) integrates with Ur's family. Ur takes the youth on an expedition to teach hunting skills. Without warning, a wild beast attacks and kills the youth, before Ur can repel it.

Ur senses a painful void, a loss of wholeness. Michener's observations draw us close to Ur's loss: that deep, inner place where Ur holds the value of joy in belonging.

> *And the anguish that Ur knew that night – the mystery of death, the triumph of evil, the terrible loneliness of being alone, the discovery that self of itself is insufficient – is the anxiety that torments the world to this day.*

Interdependence was more wonderful and enriching for Ur than *"self of itself."* It brought practical benefits – a varied food supply, a mate for the daughter. The more intense impact: it opened life for fuller and more complete personal, social and spiritual well-being.

I recall discovering the power of interdependence quite inadvertently. It was a history class needed to meet an elective requirement for my BA degree. The name of the course: "American Social and Economic History." I went to the opening class ready for a bombardment of dates and geographic data. I was so wrong. I left that session determined never to miss a class all year!

Lectures caught us up in the clash of immigrants' wide-ranging anticipations and rough conditions in this new world. Peoples' hopes and expectations were real, but ideal. Goals were determined thoughtfully and obstacles dealt with sensibly. Their insights, energy, resources, and options were neither abstract nor two-dimensional. Settlers eventually became citizens.

The course followed the settlers' story: people with ethnic, religious, and social differences striving to discover and define a shared culture. The professor engaged us in the play of local and regional dynamics. We students identified with the pressures of difficult conditions baffling hopes and expectations. Every lecture engaged me totally and motivated me to come with all my faculties alert.

Now after almost 250 years as a sovereign people, their ancestors add to the story. We deal with different problems but try to identify and focus on the common good. Healthy relationships remain vital among individuals and groups. A key element is the self each brings to relationships. The closer a relationship, the fuller self each shares. When part of self is withdrawn/withheld, the 'neighbor' experiences unease.

I've lived in a senior retirement community for over 15 years. (Four of those years I did pastoral care in a large – and swiftly "graying" – urban congregation. A retired senior soon recognizes America's fast-moving, mechanized culture orients to efficiency. This standard ripples beyond the workplace; it shapes identity, lifestyle patterns, and relationships. Refined technical skill takes precedence over personal interaction.

Behavior patterns change. Seniors feel the effect; many feel their faculties are obsolete. Most seniors try to accommodate new modes/trends, often awkwardly. (The fifth-grader handles "devices" more adeptly!) It affects one's spiritual life.

Mechanisms produce real, visible results (like email messages), but most of us don't understand the nonvisible processes that make it happen. Subtly, the less visible "spiritual" seems unreal, more abstract, two-dimensional. Power for handheld technologies relies on implanted rechargeable batteries, not an eternal, external source. Earth's horizontal reality has little need for heaven's vertical input. Spirit is about group enthusiasm and football celebrations rather than wellness of the soul.

Jesus alerts us about separating soul and self. This is what "gospel" is about. The good news centers on a single grand action: God's initiative to engage with the human self (soul and all that comes with it). It's an earth-time/space encounter with covenant bonding – an exchange. We renew rightness and wholeness in life and in life beyond death.

Israel's old covenant leaders miss the essence of this. Then along comes a Pharisee from Tarsus – Saul. Grace – God's initiative – effects a change: Saul becomes Paul. Wondrously, Paul's cultural nurturing endows him with unique skills: 1) see the value of God's initiatives for every "self," and 2) experience dynamics that bring God's initiatives into life's complex mix – cultural, spiritual.

Paul's unique message/experience/insight/revelation: God's recreative energy comes to us. Our wills bond with God's will; faith aligns our initiatives with God's (batteries included!). Faith makes spiritual real. It's a soul experience, more than a thought experience.

James Michener makes audible the value and beauty of inter-dependent relationships. History lectures made audible the yearnings and conditions settlers faced in a quest for new community. Jesus makes God visible. Paul makes God audible.

These *Meditations* are biblical exploration. The goal: experience a fresh self *in Christ*. This defines present life ... and life beyond death. New life does not isolate us from earth-life, nor does it make us passively dependent on God. The essence of covenant is interdependence. We are not equal with God but stewards entrusted with God's initiatives (God's will) in our world – however large/limited for a senior's circumstances.

As you read each *Meditation,* sense yourself in the Lord's presence – with <u>all</u> your faculties alert. Don't be detached. Don't set yourself apart because of present circumstances. Expect a supportive encounter. Don't "read" material just as information; "hear" the Spirit communing with your soul.

The English Bible versions I use are mainly: **The New Revised Standard Version** (1989) and Eugene H. Peterson's *The Message* (2005). (Throughout the book, *The Message* is indicated with "Peterson" following the scripture citation.) They provide clarity, fair parallels to original languages, and valid current American usage.

The enterprise intends for you to feel secure in abundant life now. It has continuity in life beyond death.

God, my shepherd....
true to your word,
you let me catch my breath
and send me in the right direction.

Psalm 23:1, 3
The Message,
by Eugene Peterson

Prepare for the Experience

September 1960, my first day of classes at New Brunswick Theological Seminary established by the Reformed Church in America (formerly the Dutch Reformed Church) in 1784. The Dutch settlers considered properly trained clergy a necessity, a priority for the growing number in the New York/New Jersey area.

It was midmorning chapel. A professor was leading the service. He announced the biblical text lesson – book, chapter, verses. Many fellow first-year students hurriedly opened their Bibles and began turning to the announced passage. "Please close your Bibles and set them aside," requested the professor. Students quietly followed the instruction – some bemused, all alert. The professor, looking directly and clearly at us students, said: "Hear the Word of God." It was the first time I had heard such a directive in a worship service. No others reacted, but I got ready to "Hear!"

Half the first-year class was from Iowa and Michigan and had grown up following Scripture lessons read during services. In Reformed tradition, the Scripture reading in any service is announced, then before it is read the pastor says: "Hear the Word of God." I was the only Methodist in my class – another was a senior. We both had permission to attend a non-Methodist seminary for travel reasons. We had Methodist student appointments in New Jersey parishes.

A scheduled class for first-year students followed chapel – with that professor. He explained his request. "I am aware many of you practice following the lesson in your Bibles as the pastor reads. I think it is important for all to *"hear"* what is read rather than try to read and listen simultaneously."

The image struck a chord with me. Years in elementary school, high school, undergraduate, and postgraduate studies encouraged me to use all available sense inputs to maximize learning. The Reformed Church tradition does not deny this, but it underscores a great benefit from concentrating on one sense input at a time. (For more than 50 years now, whenever I prepare to read Scripture in a public service I encourage those gathered: "Hear the Word of God.")

"Hear!" It wasn't new in 1960, or 1784. Go back to Isaiah and Jeremiah, go back to Moses: *"Hear, O Israel: the Lord is our God, the Lord alone. You shall love the Lord your God with all your heart, and with all your soul, and with all your might. Keep these words...."* (Deuteronomy 6:4-5a)

"Hear the Word of God" underscores the prophetic element in a pastoral ministry. It channels spiritual energy of God's Word to a sermon. The experience bonds presentation and hearing of Scripture truth expounded. The Word thus initiates and stimulates a richer response. It wakens a "now" moment of spiritual discovery. It moves beyond "message" to the grandeur of a fresh encounter with divine presence.

Israel's prophets – major and minor – indicate a pattern. Each describes a particular "now" in the stream of history and its unrightness in direction, in behaviors. Then each makes a significant shift to promises: a way to reconcile forces of despair to become forces of hope. For the prophet it is not nature that is out of joint, it is our human story, our history. The prophet perceives covenant history has lost is equilibrium, its poise.

"Hear" God's right *vis-à-vis* observed unright. This is to trust God's "realness." It is called faith. Reorientation to live by God's "realness" is love. Faith initiates my own service of love, and that generates hope. This sequence of initiatives (faith, love, hope) shows how to live compatibly with the Presence. It is positive transition of my action, my behavior, my initiatives. Isaiah earlier called Israel to "hear" more about the Word of God: *"...so shall my word be that goes out from my mouth, it shall not return to me empty, but it shall accomplish that which I purpose, and succeed in the thing for which I sent it."* (Isaiah 55:11)

Before and behind and around all this call to *"Hear"* is another experience – God's visibility. God had shown himself on Sinai. Centuries later, at the right time, angels called to shepherds on Bethlehem's hillsides and bade them *"listen," "hear"* – good news. It announced Emmanuel's presence, God-with-us in person, in action. In due course, the risen/ascended Christ came again: Presence as the indwelling Holy Spirit. Thus, an assurance: Faith abides, love abides, hope abides.

I am a senior now, well past my three score and 10 years. I reflect on "my history," more pointedly, my spiritual history. I have time and a desire to do that. I want faith, love, and hope to be living in my story. I desire their influence on my integrity and completeness. I want assurance I walk in the Light, sense the grandeur of God's presence in me and in my service.

Approach this material with two perspectives: Devotion and Meditation. Devotion is the collection of materials that shape and refine our commitments. These insights and truths integrate thought, emotion, action. It makes whole the soul/spirit – what shapes: 1) our identity, 2) the self we share in relationships, 3) the self that knows God and God knows. Devotional materials – hymns, poetry, Scripture – prepare us rightly for meditation on how these make us whole and holy.

Meditation is energy focused on a topic, an objective. It lifts us beyond our usual thoughts and digressions. It opens the soul to fuller communion. For example: to meditate on faith focuses my response to God's revelation.

We get ready for every new venture – a holiday trip, a reunion, an exploration. This venture is not to look at natural scenery; rather, we update the album of major elements that form our spiritual life. So, it's helpful to determine what makes up our spiritual life thus far – then explore.

Our topics are: faith, love, and hope. What in our life story during these years indicates these topics are important, clear, empowering? It's time to expose self to the fullness of life Jesus brings. Prepare by reviewing the key elements forming your spiritual life. ***Meditations One – Eleven*** touch on standard themes Jesus' followers *"Hear"* and act on.

Meditation One

Preparing for Mystery

In the beginning when God created the heavens and the earth, the earth was a formless void and darkness covered the face of the deep, while a wind from God swept over the face of the waters. Then God said.... (Genesis 1:1-2, 3a)
In the beginning was the Word, and the Word was with God, and the Word was God. He was in the beginning with God. All things came into being through him, and without him not one thing came into being. (John 1:1-3)
And the one who was seated on the throne said, "See, I am making all things new...I am the Alpha and the Omega, the beginning and the end."

(Revelation 21:5a, 6a)

My wife, Sylvia, and I prepared for missionary service in New Delhi, India. We were alerted to new climate conditions: very hot and dry season, very humid and wet monsoon season, pleasant – even cold – other season. We gathered and packed clothing for personal needs in these categories. We arrived in India at the beginning of the hot season and adapted to changes as they came.

After passing through a 12-month cycle of Delhi's seasons, we were aware of certain feelings, energies we associated with seasons. We particularly missed North American autumn – how it stirs creative thinking/planning and energizes activities. Oh yes, the leaves of the *neem* tree in our front garden fell in the hot season – no change of color, just new leaves pushing dried ones to fall. No chilly brisk winds.

Our second October in India was nearing, and we decided to take a week's holiday in the valley of Kashmir. The road journey over the Himalayas would require three days each way by bus; we could fly from Delhi and reach Srinagar in one and a half hours. We arranged the air travel. A friend suggested accommodation on a houseboat moored in Nagin Lake, outside Srinagar; we booked that. We read up on places of interest in the valley. We perspired even as we packed sweaters.

It was wonderful. *Chinar* tree leaves were changing color. Humidity was low. Evenings were nippy, and mornings had mist rising from the still, warm lake water. We enjoyed the sights. We were autumn-energized!

We returned to Kashmir in many other Octobers and enjoyed its "change of season." But these revisitations were treasured for their "inner" impact. It was no longer a trip for visual discovery. We were drawn to the valley by the season's aliveness and beauty. It was what the experience got out of us, more than what we got out of the place. Enchantment: the lavish colors of flowers in terraced Moghul gardens, lotuses blooming in secluded waterways, the encircling snow-topped Himalayan peaks. All of it renewed, revived. Each revisit affected us – mentally, aesthetically, spiritually.

As a senior, I reflect on my treasure of spiritual experience; I find I tend to generalize – beliefs, cherished biblical references, fine speakers, stirring challenges, opportunities for witness and service. I recall what is encouraging; much of it is a bit hazy and distant.

I don't have the energy, vitality, or opportunity to revisit all those experiences, and such a venture seems unnecessary, even irrelevant. What I can do is explore key elements I want to "reown" – clearly, not vaguely.

Ownership of these elements is a transforming engagement. It lasts – in life and death and life beyond death.

These elements are ours when we experience life *in Christ*. This brings completeness. Paul notes three key elements that "abide" – faith, hope, love. In translating Paul's words, "abide" indicates continuity, constancy, resolving to a perfected state/intent. Its rightness carries in and through time, in and through space as we know them.

Look again at the biblical passages above on the title page of this *Meditation*. They speak of the God's creative energy – the winds (spirit) of eternity, time, and space open to past, present, future. Those *in Christ* move on this wind/spirit of eternity, this blessing of faith, hope, love. If we (especially as seniors) dwell only in "self," we are left grasping our present, and the winds/spirit of eternity move on.

In a "present" time some 2,000 years ago, God's energy gave us Jesus' resurrection. It affirms God as Lord and Spirit abides. Note Jesus' words (from *The Message*, Eugene Peterson's translation of the Bible):

> *"The Holy Spirit whom the Father will send at my request, will make everything plain to you. He will remind you of all the things I have told you."* (John 14:26)
> *"When the Friend I plan to send you from the Father comes – the Spirit of Truth issuing from the Father – he will confirm everything about me."* (John 15:26)

This recreative, ongoing work clearly includes us in God's life and purposes. Jesus claims this when he begins his ministry (after the arrest of John the Baptist):

> *"The time is fulfilled, and the kingdom of God has come near; repent, and believe in the good news."* (Mark 1:15)

A short time later, Jesus is teaching a crowd by the Sea of Galilee. He gets in a boat and moves out from the shore so the crowd can see and hear. He speaks a parable of the sower going to the field and sowing seed. The seed falls onto various "soils": some untilled, some rocky, some full of weeds, and most of it ready to receive and nurture seed. The seed falling in the latter produces 30-, 60-, 100-fold.

Jesus begins the parable with an imperative call: *"Listen!"* It is not a request to keep quiet; it is an eastern way of calling attention to an action close to one's own experience. Indeed, Jesus' hearers were aware of success and shortfall in ordinary farming. (We return to this parable in **Meditation Five**.)

Jesus' call *"Listen!"* challenges us not to stand outside the activity, be onlookers, "observers" of what involves others. Jesus doesn't describe a puppet-drama diverting us. No! His parable is a happening in which "hearers" are participants. It affects and influences your actions and your choices. In essence, Jesus says God's action comes to each hearer. God is sowing seed; each is the soil – what kind? All are engaged in the seed's future.

A faith encounter calls for a transition from observer to participant. It is a call to get out of the grandstands and into the arena. Don't look at "it" happening *out there,* but experience the happening within. A seed dies in the soil, gets new life, ripens.

As seniors, we bring with us many ideas bundled as "faith." The following **Meditations** address topics, themes in our faith memory bank. We note key themes along with particular insights we recall and recollect.

This lays the ground for "explorations" in three topics: faith, love, hope. Our purpose is to discover more forcefully and positively how these abide and engage us. Perhaps up to this point in time we think of "faith, love, and hope" as a comforting motto taken from 1 Corinthians 13. The exploration makes them living encounters of God-with-us – not abstractly or as onlookers.

Think of the image of "sound." We hear sound, and we can distinguish various sources. A door slams shut in the wind. A glass falls and breaks on a hard surface. A baby "coos" as it is cradled. An uncontrollable sob of one lost in grief. In music it is possible to recognize sound from a trumpet, or an electric guitar, or an oboe, or a harp. Many sources, many causes – but they merge so we hear one sound, always a unique sense experience.

Rabindranath Tagore, the Nobel Prize-winning Indian poet/writer composed verses titled "Crossing." They address a spiritual union of the human and divine. Verse LXVIII expresses the unity as sound/light, Word/Presence.

There are numerous strings in your lute, let me add my own among them.
Then when you smite your chords my heart will break its silence and my life will be one with your song.
Amidst your numberless stars let me place my own little lamp,
In the dance of your festival of lights my heart will throb and my life will be one with your smile.

The exploration involves a transition, a change. Hopefully, a discovery of your life more clearly *in Christ*. It is a loss of a life as "self"; it is life redeemed – yours in God's time/space.

In the words of Jesus (Mark 1:15 above) is the phrase: "...*the kingdom of God has come near....repent.*" Note the order. First, God's initiative, then our response. Salvation comes first, then repentance. Repentance does not create salvation; repentance shows we accept, lay hold of, salvation.

The free outpouring of God's love is grace. Grace is being "found" – usually long before we are aware of what our "lostness" is.

We begin with recollections of our "faith." Then exploration gives the seed new life in grace-full soil.

This seems a mystery to many....belonging to some other time and space. But it is not hidden in a future surprise event. This faith opens the mystery of God's activity already taking place in and among us.

Draw Me Nearer

Then I saw a new heaven and a new earth...and a voice saying: "See, the home of God is among mortals, he will dwell with them as their God; they will be his peoples, and God himself will be with them... See, I am making all things new."

(Revelation 21:3, 5b)

As the deer longs for flowing streams, so my soul longs for you, O God. My soul thirsts for God, for the living God. When shall I come and behold the face of God? My tears have been my food day and night, while people say to me continually, "Where is our God?" Why are you cast down, O my soul, and why are you disquieted within me? Hope in God; for I shall again praise him, my hope and my God. (Psalm 42:1-3, 11)

It is New Year's Day, the first of January. January is named for the Roman god Janus, a two-faced deity. One face looks back on what has been; one face peers toward what lies before. Janus symbolizes the dynamic continuity of experience, reality – past, present, future. Janus – 2,000-year-old image of discontinuity/continuity – end is beginning.

In my senior years, I don't stay up to "ring in" a boisterous, midnight-hour New Year's Eve transition. However, I do reflect on what in the past year affected my life story, well-being, events, and relationships. Some of my reflections are magnificent, some less joyful.

The progression of senior years makes my "world" less expansive and varied. I move less agilely, even more carefully in unfamiliar places. I am mindful there are fewer chairs in my circle of cherished friends and associates. I remember joyfully, sadly, ones now gone on to greater glory.

The writer of Psalm 42 names a familiar senior feeling: *disquieted*. It's an unsettledness, restlessness of the spirit; something disturbs my inner serenity – and there is no medication to ease it. The psalmist looks back for an explanation: *"Why?"* The psalmist peers ahead to hear an empowering reply: *"Hope in God."*

Our spiritual encounter with Jesus infuses a new dynamic in the transition of end-beginning. It is *hope in God* ... not just recognition of time-change, but energy for life-change. It bids us *"ponder anew what the Almighty can do."*

T.S. Eliot writes of the experience in the "Little Gidding," part of his *Four Quartets* (1942):

> *What we call the beginning is often the end*
> *and to make an end is to make a beginning.*
> *We shall not cease from exploration*
> *and the end of all our exploring*
> *will be to arrive where we started*
> *and know the place for the first time.*

It is New Year's Day. I run through the pages of my Month-at-a-Glance calendar for the year just concluded. My handwritten entries bring so much to mind. Uplifting family visits and reunions. Telephone calls/emails connecting with old friends. Spirit-lifting getaway times with my wife. Even medical appointments that didn't bring perfect health but opened a way to better vitality.

I file that calendar and take my Month-at-a Glance for the new year. I transfer collected memos as entries in waiting blank spaces. Health care appointments reach well into the 12 months ahead. Birthdays are fixed celebrations. A smile crosses my face as I note the reservation my wife and I have in Florida's warming sunshine when it is cold and dreary in our North Carolina mountains.

Disquieted! I return to the opening of the psalm and catch the impact of the image given. It is a deer in the wild, alert! There are sounds that waken caution, and more securing ones like thirst-quenching water rushing over stones in the riverbed. That is energizing, it signals waiting reprieve for disquieting thirst.

The writer of Psalm 42 is part of a pilgrim assembly going to celebrate Passover in Jerusalem.

Passover, the feast of unleavened bread, is celebration of the hasty Exodus – when Moses led the Hebrews from slavery in Egypt. The psalmist travels with his own weight of personal uneasiness: health, business, spiritual. No surprise that introspection during this long journey brings to mind such thoughts and feelings. Then another pilgrim breaks into a song of thanksgiving for God's redemptive mercies. The *disquiet*, though real, is suddenly less significant than the hope borne of faith.

T.S. Eliot connects the union of end-beginning with "exploration." Our destination is no holy site; it is inner – visiting anew our own faith moments and sources. The exploration most certainly revives revealing insights in Scripture. The expectation: to recover things heretofore missed, glossed over, unnoted.

We also draw on inspiring passages from poets and narrative writers. Literature captures valued human experience and expresses it in uplifting and relevant ways.

Read again the passage of T.S. Eliot, then read Charles Wesley's hymn *Love Divine, All Love's Excelling* (vv1, 2, 4)

Love divine, all loves excelling, joy in <u>heaven to earth come down</u>;
<u>fix in us</u> thy humble dwelling, all thy faithful mercies crown!
Jesus, thou are all compassion, pure, unbounded love thou art;
visit us with thy salvation, <u>enter</u> every trembling heart.

Breathe, O <u>breathe thy loving Spirit</u> into every troubled breast!
Let us all in thee <u>inherit</u>; let us <u>find</u> that second rest.

Take away our bent to sinning, Alpha and Omega be;
end of faith, as its beginning, set our hearts at liberty.

<u>Finish</u>, *then, thy new creation; pure and spotless let us be.*
Let us see thy great salvation perfectly <u>restored</u> in thee;
<u>changed</u> from glory into glory, till in heaven we take our place,
till we cast our crowns before thee, lost in wonder, love and praise.

I underline verbs and phrases to help fix them in our consciousness as we explore. They may address lingering *disquiet*.

Many of us visit great historic landmarks – museums, great houses, cathedrals, monuments. Tour guides identify significant features. Some extraordinary guides offer special information beyond the obvious; this adds lasting impact – "Aha" moments that make exploration glorious, uplifting.

The term "senior moments" describes embarrassing times when we fail to recall a name, a situation, an experience. It happens to many of us seniors, and it is unnerving. Any such instance alarms us that it signals the onset of the loss of a cherished skill.

This **Meditation** is titled **Draw Me Nearer**. Our concern is spiritual vitality. During this time of life – this "senior season" – we possibly encounter this feeling: *"Why are you cast down, O my soul, and why are you disquieted within me?"* This need not be the end, but the beginning: *"Hope in God."*

This exploration doesn't conclude at a finish point. We bring to mind familiar themes and topics familiar in every life story. We do some spiritual sorting: we reidentify and integrate elements of our life *in Christ* … or if we have not felt secure *in Christ,* we strive to confirm the blessing. A senior season is a time to rejoice in fellowship of God-with-us. We remember <u>how</u> God is with us. We choose to let God's initiative draw us nearer. And we begin with less clutter.

Before we are ready and set to begin the explorations, we gather our own equipment, our spiritual resources – many remembered, some only faintly. These are essential elements of our spiritual "self," foundation stones (rocks of faith) gathered in our past – one face of Janus. The following **Meditations** refresh key spiritual topics that undergird our exploration of faith, love, hope – the other face of Janus.

Meditation Three

"You Will Follow Afterward"

Jesus said: "Where I am going, you cannot follow me now; but you will follow afterward....I will come again and take you to myself, so that where I am, there you may be also. And you know the way to the place where I am going...I am the way, and the truth, and the life." (John 13:36b; 14:3-4, 6)

It was another gray February morning in 1938. For the fifth or sixth time, I rubbed away the fog my breath formed on the frigid windowpane. My eyes sought out the brilliant whiteness of "heaven." My forearm cleared the haze, and again the image was clear – Hurffville Grammar School (across the road, a five-minute walk) an image of this little boy's "heaven."

I was a few months more than 4 years old. No other children my age lived in the few houses at our village crossroads. During autumn months I entertained myself contentedly outdoors and inside the house. Now I was housebound and tired of building things with Lincoln Logs and Tinkertoys. My older brother spent his days in "heaven" in the first-grade class. Mother's days were full caring for my 3-week-old sister. Dad was pastor of a sprawling rural Methodist parish in southern New Jersey. At that window I picture myself in "heaven" among other housebound playmates.

I pestered my parents: "Let me go to school." They explained the requirement (many times!): Admission is possible only in September after my next birthday. Then I would be old enough. I persisted.

My father talked – pleaded!?!?!? – with Miss Scott, the kinder-garten/first-grade teacher. (She was my Sunday school teacher; she knew my competence level and behavior patterns with other children.) It was agreed I could be in kindergarten (provisionally) in September 1938, three months before my fifth birthday. I must demonstrate physical/mental/emotional readiness comparable with others in the class group. I needed a vaccination for smallpox. (Small price for "hope.")

On Wednesday following Labor Day, the school bell tolled, the doors opened, and I skipped down the corridor. I was "high" with confidence and excitement. I explored the classroom space and furnishings. Classmates compared vaccination marks – our badges of admission.

It never occurred to me it was an end to life in my own little world. I entered an ever-expanding human journey: fuller identity, enlarged community, shared actions aiding or hindering outcomes. Beginning life in this "heaven" was prelude for many birth-to-death transitions, in many spaces shared with ever-changing sets of fellow sojourners.

Growing up (individual development) is more than a private matter. Admission to school means I become part of a community – persons interacting. I integrate with others, and together we discover both common traditions and personal horizons. Each learns how to share and support and sustain something greater than the sum of individual parts. In this complex context we discover how to 1) appreciate individual gifts and talents, 2) share strengths, and 3) reap mutual benefits.

That first day of school was a seed moment. From that came a lifelong progression of fulfillments and transitions. We recognize these particularly in relationships and interpersonal responsibilities. They happen more subtly in one's inner, spiritual self.

My lifeline now moves fast-forward some 60 years to 1998. My wife and I retire from almost 40 years of missionary service in India and other parts of Asia. A missionary journey begins more circuitously than admission to Hurffville Grammar School. It starts as conversations with Methodist Board of Missions' staff. Their purpose is to assess compatibility of applicants with mission field needs and conditions. The next step: determine a right "fit" of our qualifications and gifts with a mission field "call" (need). Assessment of this "rightness" is apt and assuring. Once a partnering emerges clearly, the Mission Board prepares candidates for commissioning and departure for the field.

Sylvia and I felt competent and confident to fulfill India's stated need: "Church Development"… as open-ended as that phrase (and concept) was then. The specific appointment: establish a congregation for a newly constructed church building in an emerging New Delhi suburb. The less obvious element was the spiritual change and transition that we were entering, and how that might shape us for a wider range of service.

Hindsight makes clear the inner transition begins with our 1964 arrival in India. It was a subtle end-beginning to identity as spiritual beings. The obvious part was new ways of living-serving. The less obvious (more hidden) meanings were changed perspectives and reformed behavior correct for a new cultural environment. The transition was surprisingly smooth from the beginning. Mission Board orientation programs resolved many questions and demystified much about the new context.

Our first home leave in the USA (after more than five years away) was eye-opening! Visible change in America abounded: new products, new styles, new measures of "must have." We observed these with interest and amazement, always aware we were "visiting." We would be in the States for three months, then reengage again in our real life in New Delhi. These "differences" in the USA didn't really touch what was now important in our life/service. The more lasting personal value of the home leave was reconnection with family, friends, and church congregations committed to our missionary work.

Return from home leave confirms how truly our Delhi/India appointment is home. Mind and body and spirit are not in cultural conflict, they harmonize: who we are and what we do and where we are. This home is different from the one we had grown up in. Our calling places us on a way less traveled – a new road/way, different but spiritually right. Robert Frost's lines comes to mind:

> *Two roads diverged in a wood, and I –*
> *I took the one less traveled by,*
> *and that has made all the difference.*

The change requires our full attention and energy. It is not more perfect than our American context, but it is right.

Our Indian colleagues openly include us as seasoned partners – not interns, not outsiders. The Indian church's goals are our goals; our missionary gifts and graces integrate smoothly to further local/national goals. We frequently negotiate procedures but share a known purpose.

Those decades of service happened in real time and space; life and service was not fantasized as something in a "let's pretend" heaven. Real life in real contexts – always grounded in spiritual authenticity … almost always matching expectations. At retirement gatherings our service is recognized.

Again, the story moves fast-forward (a briefer time span) to life as a senior. Retirement life expectations blend optimism and undercurrents of fear. There is the optimism of release from work agendas, return to the reality of our birth culture. There is fear of unforeseen changes and unpleasant limitations: deteriorating health, reduced mobility, slowing mental agility. We minimize involuntary shifts in what is called "normal" (outlook, responsiveness, participation) – anything that affects how we handle space, relationships, esteem – at home or anywhere. Capabilities decrease, and losses increase.

Then come those "senior moments." (We smile but fear their frequency and unpredictability.) Instant recall is less deft – loosed from memory's magnetic hold. We cope with slight lapses. We dread a chronic disconnect from skills that tie us to others, our own identity. We slip – not into another world, but toward a "no" world: no who, no what, no when, no where, no why, no how. Genetic makeup and a less demanding lifestyle add to aging.

So, do we lapse into spiritual inertia? A Christian should not! We are biologically older, but reset our identity by nonbiological norms. We inaugurate a new spiritual exercise regimen and discover gifts, initiatives of redeemed spiritual DNA. Benefits await and are accessible. It's time to clear blurry vision (and hearing) – especially so heaven is allowed its own identity.

We seniors have more time. We leave career agendas. We turn over leadership commitments (often not easy but positive and possible). It's an opportunity to test and reform appropriate goals. We appreciate recognitions and honors for contributions and achievements, but are content to leave them in their intended time frame. We retire earth-life trophies; we turn them over as thank-offerings for past stewardship, bequeath them as part of a heritage.

A key issue is time. Creative pre-retirees consider new options. Pursue a fresh agenda directed to beckoning light, perhaps involving other ways/roads. Reject a vague, dark tunnel of "same old-same old" patterns that diminish your identity. Review your spiritual biography … that assortment of elements that shape your faith identity. Consider resources you neglected, thought irrelevant. Make them important for a continuing life-story.

Search out what awaits your stewardship. Retirement may change your obligations, but your service is not neutralized. Open yourself positively to participate in life up to and beyond death – do it without morbidity, regularly updating your capacities. Identify timeless assets in your spirit-treasure. These will energize new goals. Reclaim talents and graces forgotten or left partially developed. No stamp "invalid" looms over senior years. A spiritual being is a *"good and faithful steward"* (Matt 25:21) in all this human experience. Your cache of spirit-riches doesn't dissolve into dust and ashes. Literally, we seniors are closer to heaven than ever before! It is time to revive and grasp the spiritual realities that help us live up to and beyond death.

End of childhood development. End of adult-measured productivity. Beginning of life in transition … this time it's very personal, but not exclusive or private. There is a new priority: it is now kingdom-time … the kingdom Jesus speaks of – God's sway, involvement and priority in grander space, less measured time. We are already part of this kingdom, and its fullness is already prepared. How ready are we to be "home"?

Meditation Four

Getting Outside the Box

Jesus is with his close followers and says to them:
"You've been given insight into God's kingdom – you know how it works. But to those who can't see it yet, everything comes in stories, creating readiness, nudging them toward receptive insight. These are people whose eyes are open but don't see a thing, whose ears are open but don't understand a word, who avoid making an about-face and getting forgiven."   (Mark 5:11-12, Peterson)

In the 1970s and 1980s management consultants challenged clients to "think outside the box." Edward de Bono introduced the idea of "lateral thinking" in 1967; his focus was solving problems. A usual practice for problem-solving is advancing step-by-step in a logical sequence; de Bono's alternative encourages a different pattern: step laterally ("sideways"). This shift explores new horizons for a solution.

The concept "thinking outside the box" visualizes the idea as a diagram of nine dots arranged in a symmetrical square. Directions: Link all nine dots using four straight lines or fewer, without lifting the pencil and without tracing the same line more than once.

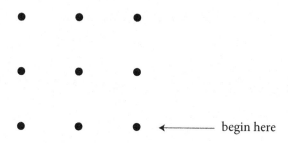

A solution: Let some lines extend outside the presumed confines of the "box" the nine dots define.

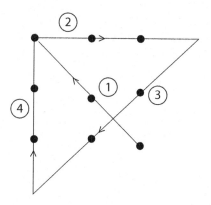

This exercise deals with physical space. But it reminds us how often we confine understanding to presumed mental boundaries, e.g., perceiving words only in a literal sense. For example, refer to the passage from Mark on the previous page, and Jesus' choice of the word "eyes." "Sight" enables 1) the brain to identify a physical object (e.g., an oak tree), and 2) the brain can "see" that same object symbolically as strength and stability (e.g., as in the phrase, a "mighty oak"). Jesus uses "eye" in the passage for both sight and insight, i.e., defining and interpreting of reality.

Many of us experience this layered meaning of literal and symbolic language as an impact of proverbs. The Bible devotes an entire book to proverbs lauding "wisdom" – knowing the long-term nature of God's purposes. Here is an example (Proverbs 2:1-5):

> *My child, if you accept my words and treasure up my command-ments within you, making your ear attentive to wisdom and inclining your heart to understanding; if you indeed cry out for insight, and raise your voice for understanding; if you seek it like silver, and search for it as for hidden treasures – then you will understand the fear of the Lord and find knowledge of God.*

"Wisdom" here is used on two levels: a mental achievement and an encounter. It speaks to the mind, yes, but also the soul and spirit.

A year or two after being in India, we attended an annual church conference. One evening's program recognized three members who were retiring. (Presentations were in Hindi and Urdu.) For two of the honorees speeches were given – abounding in glorious adjectives about their gifts and achievements. The third was honored with a traditional Indian form: a sung lyric of rhyming couplets.

Sylvia and I managed the local language in prose form, but sung poetic imagery was more elusive, especially the Eastern tradition of florid, exaggerated expression. (The ear must catch quickly both a word and its poetic nuances.) Through our years in India we handled this kind of experience more adeptly and so discovered beauty and impact inherent in the form.

In this ancient poetic tradition there is no special, elevated "voca-bulary"; words are common in everyday, down-to-earth daily life. The shift from everyday prose to poetic expression happens naturally, easily. In this tradition, poetic images say two things at once to intensify emotional and spiritual impact. Life events so shared reveal layers of meaning and heighten impact. This does more than excite us; it sharpens our perception of what is important and beautiful. The impact: shared information, testimony and a stimulating encounter – the hearer with the poem's inner soul/spirit.

Jesus' communication (and Old Testament prophets' as well) often implies more than a literal sense. Careful attention indicates more and profound meanings, commonly described as "hidden meanings." A hidden meaning is not secretive or misleading; rather, full impact calls for a special commitment/investment of the hearer – a faith investment. And this is not unique to biblical writing.

In *The Collected Prose of Robert Frost,* edited by Mark Richardson, Lawrence Thompson notes a comment Robert Frost made in a talk (1983):

> *[Frost] said that in writing a poem, he was aware of saying two things at once; but wanting to say the first thing so well that any reader who liked that part of the poem might feel free to settle for that part of the poem as sufficient in itself. But, he added, it was of the nature of poetry to say two things at once, and it was of the nature of literary appreciation to perceive that an ulterior meaning had been included in the particular meaning.*

Note: Frost's use of "ulterior" is a bit obscure, confusing. Frost indicates the additional meaning (perhaps figurative or "hidden") expands options for the poet and the reader.

Frost's poem *Mending Walls* begins: *Something there is that doesn't love a wall.* Frost observes this on arrival at the boundary between his field and a cherished neighbor's field. The neighbor joins Frost to reset stones fallen in winter weather. As they work the neighbor says: *"Fences make good neighbors."* This particular use of "wall/fence" widens meaning: 1) property boundary, and 2) personal boundaries neighbors honor when they interact.

Our explorations bring us face-to-face with conversations and teachings of Jesus and his contemporaries. We open our minds and spirits to layers and dimensions in the words/phrases that are true and carry a spiritual impact for us. Living in Eastern cultures helped us be comfortable with "layers" of meaning.

Our Western heritage (with its Greek and Roman cultural roots) tends to present ideas in "boxes" in order to keep the measure of clarity as particular as possible. Logical and figurative expression do not generally overlap (except in idiomatic and "slang" expressions).

Jesus' use of parables (a very ordinary Eastern pattern) is not to set "in" and "out" groups in contention. It offers understanding that reaches varying levels of readiness (both mind and soul/spirit). This opens the kingdom experience for a wider audience. Exploration opens multiple layers/dimensions of spiritual reality, to wholeness and holiness.

Meditation Five

Kingdom Time

After John [the Baptist] was arrested Jesus went to Galilee preaching the message of God: "Time's up! God's kingdom is here. Change your life and believe the message." (Mark 1:14-15, Peterson)
Jesus, grilled by the Pharisees on when the kingdom of God would come, answered, "The kingdom of God doesn't come by counting the days on the calendar. Nor when someone says, 'Look here!' or 'There it is!' And why? Because God's kingdom is already among you." (Luke 17:20-21, Peterson)

The Hebrew, Aramaic and Greek words translated as "kingdom" in English Bibles are part of everyday language for teachers of Jewish law. "Kingdom" is a major feature in the peoples' history. It describes the human power governing designated territory and the institutions that control its activity.

The heirs of Abraham, Isaac, and Jacob were in Egypt as slaves. After hundreds of years, God delivered them (the Exodus). They reached their own "promised land" and modeled their governance on familiar, neighboring patterns – friendly and otherwise. About 1000 B.C., heroic kings Saul, David, and Solomon stabilized Israel's political identity (and pride!).

The eastern Mediterranean basin was perpetually unstable politically. Israel was overrun by the forces of King Nebuchadnezzar of Babylon and taken into exile. This became tangled with Persian expansion. After some years, King Cyrus allowed some exiled Jews to return and rebuild Jerusalem. Sometime later, Persia, under Xerxes I, took control of the territory. By the time of Jesus' birth, authority shifted to the Roman Empire. Control of the "promised land" was always in transition.

Israel's story – the peoples' shared biography – cherished the vision of its own kingdom. It was a memory passed from the Patriarchs to all succeeding generations: God gave and would restore the kingdom and be present as their God.

Back in 538 B.C. when Cyrus allowed a remnant to return to Jerusalem, the prophetic figures of Ezra and Nehemiah called for a new obedience to the Law. The priestly figures in the community interpreted the Law more basically; religious scholars and leaders monitored adherence. "Rightness" became a more literal reading of the Law.

In this context the anticipated kingdom was expressed in new terms. One group expected the appearance of a messianic figure who would restore Israel's fortunes. Another group had more cosmic expectations, something apocalyptic. It would be a singular event – a cataclysmic upheaval ending in victory and judgment: a new city of God would descend with God himself dwelling in it. Upholders of the Law would be honored; the unfaithful would be doomed. It would end changes belonging to time and space.

Jesus is born. Hastily, Hebrew scholars seek scriptural explanations for Jesus' actions and behavior. A questioning ensues: Does Jesus fulfill the expected messianic role? Is he the beginning of the end? John the Baptist, in prison, sends followers to inquire of Jesus if this is the time of the expected kingdom. Jesus shifts attention from political to personal transformations:

"Go and tell John what you hear and see: the blind receive their sight, the lame walk, the lepers are cleansed, the deaf hear, the dead are raised, and the poor have good news brought to them. And blessed is anyone who takes no offense at me."

(Luke 7:22-23)

"Blessed" – God's rule, God's work, comes to you. This rule, this work, it is a happening **in you**, it involves you, affects you. ("Affect" is an inner action; God's involvement in your life alters the way you believe, take initiative, serve, act. It repositions your perspective on life and toward others. You no longer hold the attitude of a spectator. You are "in" the action, and the action is "in" you.)

In Mark, Jesus' initial teaching uses parables about seeds and sowing. We note these briefly (all from Mark, chapter four).

1) The sower scatters seed. a) Some falls on a trodden path – birds eat it. b) Some falls on rocky ground – rooting is difficult, sprouts die. c) Some falls among thorns and weeds, which choke new sprouts. d) Some falls on good ground (i.e., soil readied to receive and nurture seed) – this yields 30-, 60-, 100-fold.

In rural India in 1964, there was little mechanization. Plowing was done by paired oxen. Sowing was done by hand. Harvest was a manual operation. The irregular shape and size of arable plots had common characteristics: The area of good soil was carefully plowed and readied for seed. Each had a boundary of: a) footpaths with packed-down soil, b) edges of scattered stone and rock brought out of the arable area during plowing, c) borders where thorns, weeds, tares flourished in bits of untilled soil. The farmer sowed seed with a sweeping gesture – casting the seed in a large arc as he walked up and down the field. Some seed landed on the edges – paths, rocks, weeds – not intentionally, but in the normal broadcasting of seed. The majority of seed fell on waiting, productive soil. (Note this, lest the passage in Mark suggest the sower was careless. A fraction for "loss" or "waste" is presumed in the process.)

2) The sower sows, leaves the field and sleeps (carries on other related tasks), and the seed sprouts, matures, and the grain ripens. The important factor is the soil prepared to receive the seed. Our calling (figuratively) is to be the kingdom's "soil." The soil fosters rebirth, renewing energy; good soil welcomes and nurtures seed it holds.

3) The "seed" – God's will – may seem insignificantly small, but inherent in that hardly visible beginning is the fullness of the fruit and the harvest.

It is important to observe how the call to "repentance" shifts from John the Baptist to Jesus. John says repent to get ready for what is coming. Jesus calls hearers to lay hold of the salvation that is at hand, now. Repentance is a decision to end a role as onlooker. God's initiative visualizes us in the arena of action. Jesus' bidding: "be perfect" (Matt 5:8) – respond to God's initiative (that response is faith).

Repentance affirms we lay hold of salvation. God's initiative precedes our initiative. *"Joy of heaven to earth come down"* is now happening; each of us is the soil for life-initiatives (more than death-finalities!). We are no longer spectators gathered on the secular side of the fence to watch and comment on action in a sacred field.

The more urgent call is recognition that the present is indeed God's present linked to God's future. The challenge: Can we free a grasp on "our present" and put ourselves in God's time? Is it because we fear judgment? Whatever judgment happens is because we choose to keep "our" own present and future separate from God's initiatives.

The most complex faith issue Jesus posed for the orthodox Jewish community was: the old covenant's more literal idea of faith and kingdom are an eroded relic of memory. Jesus' encounters with anyone – good/bad, rich/poor, outcaste/orthodox – is living faith borne in a new life.

The kingdom Jesus refers to so extensively and insistently is not a holiday destination abounding with fantasy delights. It is very up close and personal for each person. We are asked to "hear" the good news that comes; we are challenged to "see" initiatives the Lord works in and among us; we choose to be either onlookers or participants in the renewal available.

The kingdom remains a mystery when we fail to recognize it is already taking place. It is not hidden in a circuitous maze leading to an appearing-out-of-nowhere apocalypse. We are called to accept its dominion now and trust its transitions to waiting and glorious fullness.

Meditation Six

"Do You Believe This?"

Martha: Master, if you'd been here, my brother Lazarus wouldn't have died.
Even now, I know that whatever you ask God he will give you.
Jesus: Your brother will be raised up.
Martha: I know that he will be raised up in the resurrection at the end of time.
Jesus: You don't have to wait for the End. I am, right now, Resurrection and Life.
The one who believes in me, even though he [or she] dies, will live. And
everyone who lives believing in me does not ultimately die at all. Do you
believe this? (John 11:21-26, Peterson)

Matthew, Mark, and Luke each present Jesus' life in a perspective that links with Jewish tradition. The Gospel message is spreading through Asia Minor and into Europe – extending beyond Israel's heartland. The Gospel of John presents Jesus as Lord of the church. Its core impact is the Easter/ Resurrection experience and the new God-human covenant.

Many chapters in John follow a recurring pattern: 1) An action or event involving Jesus and others, e.g., water changed to wine in John 2; 2. This moves to a conversation in which Jesus clarifies the meaning of his action. Jesus draws attention to spiritual implications for life – real people, real situations. John presents Jesus in everyday-life situations and simultaneously conveys life as "real" in more than biological terms. These may have obvious **and** more hidden meanings.

The little dialogue between Martha and Jesus shows the two lines of meaning. It relates to time and space, life and death, Lazarus and Martha.

What's real for Martha is this: Her flesh-and-blood brother is lifeless. The loss is painful – at this time and in this place called Bethany. It is a hurt Martha feels deeply.

Jesus attempts to relieve that grief (and its intensity) with an assurance Lazarus *"will be raised up."* Martha tells Jesus she understands the religious teaching about resurrection as part of some future end time. It is insufficient solace that in another space at some undetermined time, the loved one she's lost here will resurrect there.

Jesus shifts the focus of relief **from** Martha's grief **to** himself and his identity. The subject shifts from loss of life to source of life. He further dissolves the absolute separation of this time/that time, this space/that space. He **is** Resurrection (the conqueror of death) and Life (the source of all vitality). The issue has cosmic scale, but Jesus gives it immediacy – a right-now, Bethany-sized issue. It comes with a direct, personal challenge: *"Martha, do you [and all of us!] believe this?"*

Martha affirms she believes. Jesus calls the dead from his tomb, and Lazarus appears, alive.

Jesus' meanings are confusing to hearers totally caught up in the situation of the moment, or when words are limited to here-now references. That signals us to look beyond the less obvious to more profound meanings – meanings relevant both now and beyond this moment. The possible "hidden" aspect is not to deceive or mislead; rather, to waken hearers' special sensitivity – a faith commitment.

So we look to implications of Jesus' designation of himself as "Resurrection and Life" (and in terms of how we perceive death).

Death is considered lifelessness: no breath, no vitality, no sense, no ability to respond. Faith adds a spiritual dimension to what we instinctively consider physical. Recall God's desire in Genesis 1:26 (Peterson's translation): *God spoke: "Let us make human beings in our image, make them reflecting our nature..."* "Our nature" suggests something other than a mirror image, a look-alike visage. It is humans' competence to respond to God's nature, to deal with God's initiatives (as a steward). This endows human life with a more-than-biological capacity for interaction, communion – covenant partnership, bonding.

Our exploration engages us in a grander experience of connections. It clearly refines our identity as spiritual beings. It helps resolve perennial questions about this human experience. Our exploration helps us understand Jesus' statement to Martha, *viz: "The one who believes in me, even though he [or she] dies, will live. And everyone who lives believing in me does not ultimately die at all."*

For the Jewish community of Jesus' day (and even among the more orthodox today) "dead" describes physical death or a person removed from fellowship – family/community (living or not). This might be a person who marries outside the community of faith; it could be a person who chooses a lifestyle outside old covenant boundaries. Anyone so separated is lost, dead. To be restored is to come alive again – in a physical and spiritual fellowship. This restoration is an act of "saving" – aliveness to God, to receive anew God's breath, to resurrect intimate union with the Lord.

Many seniors glibly self-eulogize: *"I've had a full life!"* That's so final. Why fix one's life in the past tense? State life in present/future tenses. Faith means life in all its fullness, not subject to a rationed quantity/quality or "use by" shelf-life dates. Paul heralds God's measure: life's *victory of continuity* overcomes death's *sting of discontinuity.* Resurrection *"Hallelujah!"* echoes the Christmas theme: *"Glory to God ... and peace [reconciliation] for those of goodwill."* Glorious resolution – both already experienced and not yet revealed.

Jesus in this chapter has Martha explore her faith. Jesus invites Martha to take ownership of coming alive by faith. The subject is not Lazarus' beliefs. Rather, does Martha believe Jesus is Life – now, and beyond death – not just for the brother but for herself?

A children's bedtime prayer comes to mind:

Now I lay me down to sleep,
I pray the Lord my soul to keep.
If I should die before I wake,
I pray the Lord my soul to take.

Once I came across this verse rephrased with a provocative impact:

Now I lay me down to sleep,
I pray the Lord my soul to keep.
If I should die before I live.....

Jesus' conversation with Martha calls for a leap of faith – transition from old covenant understanding to new covenant good news.

Jesus asks: *"Do you believe this?"* Those who respond positively find Jesus' identity as "Resurrection and Life" affects their identity!

Martha responds to Jesus' question positively – yes, she believes. Does that mean Martha (or any believer) now has clear answers to all matters of life and death, good and evil, belonging and separation? No. It is the basis, the sure foundation, on which a believer can trust spiritual answers for tangled human questions.

Another way of saying this is to say that faith brings us alive in a new definition of life. It is fellowship with God; it is readiness to accept and respond to God's initiatives. It is a joy of knowing this new life now and its continuity beyond death.

Our present faith – however intense it might be – energizes our exploration. None of us begins with **no** faith. The exploration will undoubtedly enrich our commitment and capacity to reflect the nature of Life God provides.

Meditation Seven

We Are Not Alone

But if God has taken up residence in your life, you can hardly be thinking more of yourselves than of him. Anyone, of course, who has not welcomed this invisible but clearly present God, the Spirit of Christ, won't know what we're talking about. But for you who welcomed him, in whom he dwells – even though you still experience all the limitations of sin – you yourself experience life on God's terms....When God lives and breathes in you (and he does, as surely as he did in Jesus), you are delivered from that dead life. With this Spirit living in you, your body will be as alive as Christ's.

(Romans 8:9-11, Peterson)

The Gospels use varied and broad strokes to help us discern the good news in Jesus' life and ministry. Jesus himself often clarifies matters. Other New Testament writers offer a treasure of ways to a fuller understanding. As the Christian community organized and expanded amid scores of cultures throughout the Roman Empire, leaders prepared creeds – statements of belief to unify the diverse community.

The most familiar of these is The Apostles' Creed. It was expanded a few centuries later as The Nicene Creed. These creeds list particular *features* of God's initiatives. Initiatives come from the three personae by which God reveals himself, his nature: Father (creator), Son (redeemer), Holy Spirit (sustainer). Collectively, these initiatives show the completeness of God's part in this human experience.

The Statement of Faith of the United Church of Canada is a 20th-century creed. Its perspective is different. It highlights *benefits* of God's initiatives that renew and redeem our human identity, witness, and service. It begins: *"We are not alone, we live in God's world."* It affirms the divine-human connection. From this we infer believers are stewards, trustees of God's intentions. This adds a major quality to our identity: Human actions are choices we accept, more than robotic obedience. Faith means our service brings God-intended outcomes into this human experience.

All these creeds refer to life beyond the time/space of our earth journey; none provide descriptive detail. Each ends differently. The Apostles' Creeds: *"...the life everlasting"* (a "time" factor). The Nicene Creed: *"...the life of the world to come"* (a "space" factor). The United Church of Canada Statement: *"In life, in death, in life beyond death, God is with us. We are not alone. Thanks be to God."* (Bonding that continues beyond earth's time and space.)

Creeds affirm God's initiatives: the Father creates, the Son redeems, the Holy Spirit sustains. Over and over Christians make these creedal affirmations. Seniors are spiritually energized by intentionally identifying benefits (fruits) of God's initiatives in their experience and lifestyle.

The phrase *"We are not alone"* impels our exploration. Life beyond death anticipates "belonging" in a thriving environment. Our present interdependence readies us for a graceful transition.

In the passage from Romans 8 given above, Paul speaks of the interinvolvement of God's life and our life. The story of Jesus – from prophetic expectations to Gospel witness to the Pentecost empowerment – elaborates on Jesus as *Emmanuel,* God-with-us. Paul uniquely perceives this divine-human bonding; he boldly asserts it in specific terms – not as theory, but experience:

> *...it is no longer I who live, but it is Christ who lives in me. And the life I now live in the flesh I live by faith in the Son of God who loved me and gave himself for me.*
>
> (Gal 2:20)

> *So if anyone is in Christ, there is a new creation: everything old has passed away; see, everything has become new!*
>
> (II Cor 5:7)

Belief here takes on a whole new dynamic. To be *"in Christ,"* or to affirm that *"Christ lives in me,"* alters the boundaries of my identity as "self." Perhaps we can understand it more aptly if we perceive life *in Christ* as in, not of, the world! And the perspective is now very different.

The new life draws people who rejoice in spiritual interdependence. It is the shepherd's way: *He leads me beside still waters; he restores my soul. He leads me in right paths for his name's sake.* (Psalm 23:2-3) This way doesn't circumvent real life. This way is characterized as one that supplies us with benefits we describe as holy, wholesome, healthful.

Seniors often find shifts to new ways discomforting. Often without warning, personal independence falters. Ready or not circumstances alter, life's conditions change. Financial security is less secure. Activity is more restricted; a life partner is lost; time/energy is inadequate to care for self. It echoes seniors' faintly remembered adolescent anxieties. We are challenged to be part of new social circles and allow unexpected partnerships to be supportive and compatible.

Consider carefully the shepherd's way: interdependence. It is a positive support for change and transition. The resources of mature faith make crises less daunting ... and we are not alone. We cope with a new goal and determine resources needed to reach it.

Crisis moments are always personal, but not necessarily unique. Few are totally original. History records a treasure store of recurring crises and positive resolutions. Literature is a wonderful resource – the Bible, biographies and fiction poignantly re-present life crises and solutions. Cherished passages relate others' experience often in contexts like our own. Go to that literature. (**I** read the literature, but more amazingly the literature reads **me**!)

Mystery and faith complete each other. Paul speaks of life both as *in Christ* and *Christ in us.* These realities belong to both mystery and faith. They open life's mechanisms to both human and spiritual energy.

Jean Anouilh reflects these dimensions in *Antigone,* his modern adaptation of Sophocles' tragedy. (Note: Anouilh's version speaks to the Free French dilemma during the Nazi occupation in World War II. The question: Should French citizens cooperate or not cooperate with the rule of Nazi invaders … in exchange for a promise of for-the-time-being benefits?).

Antigone defies King Creon's ruling and buries her rebellious brother, slain for challenging Creon's claim as king. Creon threatens his niece Antigone with death. Antigone justifies her defiance with commitment to a law higher than Creon's. Creon sets out to undermine her allegiance to higher authority.

> Creon: *You don't know what you are talking about!*
> Antigone: *I do know what I am talking about! It is you who can't hear me! I am too far away from you now, talking to you from a kingdom you can't get into.*

It's an ancient dilemma – committing to right or unright interdependence – human, spiritual. Jesus impels us to seek God's kingdom: the reign of God's right. Jesus' life and work are its surety for believers. It is a trustworthy, eternal reality. It calls for faith – a "right" interdependence. It is good seed in good soil.

Life *in Christ/Christ lives in me* is a way that undoubtedly involves change. The human changes may be bumps of discontinuity. Some cherished ways may yield to surprising alternatives. But the assurance of interdependence is grace. And grace readies us for life's transitions.

At graveside Christians affirm a transition marked by change. Paul's words: *"I tell you something wonderful, a mystery I'll probably never fully understand. We're not all going to die – but we are all going to be changed."* (I Cor 15:51-52, Peterson). The English word "change" translates the Greek <u>allagesomai</u>. It implies "to alter, to transform" – always to a different **kind** of outcome and metamorphosis from life to life.

The stabilizing and assuring element in all this is the bonding communion that comes with faith. God is with us. We are not alone.

Meditation Eight

Born of Water and of Spirit

Jesus said: "...I tell you no one can enter the kingdom of God without being born of water and Spirit. What is born of the flesh is flesh and what is born of the Spirit is spirit. Do not be astonished that I said to you, 'You must be born from above'...".
"For God so loved the world that he gave his only Son, so that everyone who believes in him may not perish but may have eternal life. Indeed, God did not send the Son into the world to condemn the world, but in order that the world might be saved through him."

(John 3:5-7, 16-17)

Luke's chapters three and four highlight four events at the beginning of Jesus' ministry:

1) Jesus' response to John the Baptist's general calling (Isaiah 40:3ff) for revival and renewal: repent and be baptized.

2) John baptizes Jesus in the Jordan River. As this baptism takes place, the Holy Spirit (in the form of a dove) alights on Jesus and a voice from above is heard saying: *"You are my Son, the Beloved, with you I am well pleased."*

3) Jesus withdraws into a wilderness to meditate on the event. He is alone; he fasts. After 40 days, he encounters the devil. The devil lures Jesus with benefits of self-aggrandizement and earthly glory. Jesus rejects these; the devil departs.

4) Jesus returns to his hometown Nazareth; at synagogue service, he reads from the prophet Isaiah (61:1-2a):

> *The Spirit of the Lord is upon me,*
> *because he has anointed me to bring good news to the poor.*
> *He has sent me to proclaim release to the blind,*
> *to let the oppressed go free, to proclaim the year of the Lord's favor.*

After reading he announces: *"Today this scripture has been fulfilled in your hearing."*

Jesus here is part of rituals long cherished in the Judeo-Christian tradition: 1) an act of cleansing – outer washing signifying inner renewal; 2) an act of anointing (or sometimes laying on of hands) – symbolizing commitment to bear a particular energy and loyalty; 3) a call: engage in a new lifestyle or new service.

When Jesus is tempted to turn stones into bread (seemingly to relieve hunger), he answers the devil with words from Deuteronomy 8:3: *"One does not live by bread alone."*

Bread is real. Hunger is real. It is common sense to accept that material provision is the solution to what we label real needs and wants. (And when we say "real," we mean tangible, physically measurable conditions.) It is understandable that scientific reality seems to have precedence over more illusory categories like spiritual. Uncommon sense moves a person to listen and understand that many elements combine for good health – body, mind, spirit.

The passage from John quoted above is from the conversation Jesus had with Nicodemus. John introduces Nicodemus with this brief bio-data: … *a Pharisee named Nicodemus, a leader of the Jews.* Nicodemus was a good man, a pillar of the religious community; he fulfilled old covenant expectations faithfully, **but**... The "but" is this: Jesus' teaching upset Nicodemus' spiritual security. Nicodemus' spiritual life suddenly seems to lack something … does it lack vitality, is it lifeless?

Compare Nicodemus' brief bio-data with another brief biography in the Bible: Enoch (Gen 5:23-24): *All the years of Enoch came to three hundred sixty-five years. Enoch walked with God then he was no more, for God took him.* The image *"walked with God"* is dynamic, it indicates bonding and continuity. It suggests fellowship, creative interdependence. It suggests a life that is more than religious correctness.

Jesus' call for new birth seemed contrary to whatever knowledge/ image Nicodemus held about how life begins (birth). Nicodemus has a literal image of physical childbirth – a one-time, nonrepeatable event. The alternative struck him as an utter impossibility. Jesus tries to open (shed light on) the subtler, spiritual, more hidden meaning: take ownership of fuller (different) life before death.

Jesus shares with Nicodemus insights about God's presence and work. He speaks of God as Spirit, moving where it will. The moving Spirit implies creative freshness, and Jesus speaks of being "born" (energized, revived) by this Spirit moving among us. It echoes the jubilant affirmation of the Psalmist (Psalm 103:1-5):

> *Bless the Lord, O my soul, and all that is within me,*
> *   bless his holy name.*
> *Bless the Lord, O my soul, and forget not all his benefits –*
> *   who forgives all your iniquity, who heals all your diseases,*
> *   who redeems your life from the Pit [death],*
> *   who crowns you with steadfast love and mercy,*
> *   who satisfies you with good as long as you live*
> *   so that your youth is renewed like the eagle's.*

I underline the word "benefits" intentionally. In any spiritual quest, it is essential to note blessings that are benchmarks in the spiritual experience. In the Judeo-Christian tradition, God is the source of true blessing. We note characteristics of God, traits we know from what is revealed, what is written of human experience. These characteristics we can label "features" of God; they are God's nature and exist whether we acknowledge them or not.

"Benefits" are what and how these features happen in us personally, collectively. A feature of God is his power and intention to forgive. The benefit is my renewing transformation when I own God's forgiveness.

To keep God's features alive in our faith is an intention of worship and devotion. To experience these as benefits is new birth. We live the newness of life.

Features become spiritually relevant when we claim them as benefits! Might that explain Nicodemus' anguish vis-à-vis Jesus' teaching of grace and love? Features are real for me when I allow them to *happen* in/with me. Jesus suggests Spirit baptism initiates *happening*!

Henry Francis Lyte gives us a great hymn of praise based on Psalm 103:

Praise, my soul, the King of heaven, to His feet thy tribute bring;
Ransomed, healed, restored, forgiven, evermore his praise sing:
Alleluia! Alleluia! Praise the everlasting King.

Underlined are beneficial actions the Lord initiates. They are not wantonly strewn about; they are fruits rising out of the soil of faith.

As a child, I had wonderful Sunday School teachers. Some were extremely caring about our young spiritual development but had a limited way of sharing their evangelical zeal and concern. I remember one in particular who taught our 6- (or 7) year-old class. Two questions were posed regularly: Were we born again, were we saved? It took several years before I could resolve that – to understand and harmonize earthly terms and spiritual experience. But in those younger years, I was totally baffled about being "saved." My childlike image of saving centered on that little piggy bank in which I dropped pennies.

A more excellent understanding of *"born of water and Spirit"* begins with grace.

Grace is renewal and reconciliation – it is creation working re-creation. Baptism's dove signals the peace (*shalom*) that comes with reconciliation.

Grace is also energy – the urgency, the Pentecostal flame, that comes with new birth in the Spirit. Here grace re-forms God's features as benefits I demonstrate in my life experience. To be *"saved"*, to be *"born again"* is the spiritual interdependence that brings holy initiatives alive in human relationships.

Grace is a resource that never ages, never wears out, never reaches a limit, never ceases to be fully personal. The most wondrous feature of grace is its surprise – it touches what we often consider untouchable!

Discern the Will of God
(the Way is the Will)

Let the same mind be in you that was in Christ Jesus, who though he was in the form of God, did not regard equality with God as something to be exploited, but emptied himself, taking the form of a slave, being born in human likeness. And being found in human likeness, he humbled himself and became obedient to the point of death – even death on a cross. Therefore God also highly exalted him and gave him the name that is above every name, so that at the name of Jesus every knee should bend, in heaven and on earth and under the earth, and every tongue should confess that Jesus Christ is Lord, to the glory of God the father.

(Philippians 2:5-11)

Do not be conformed to this world, but be transformed by the renewing of your minds, so that you may discern what is the will of God – what is good and acceptable and perfect. (Romans 12:2)

The passages cited above are Paul's guides for new covenant people in the early church. Paul's background was truly cosmopolitan: Jewish by birth, recognized Pharisee, outside Jerusalem's inner circle of new Christians, educated in a Greek environment and culture, Roman citizen. Paul's spiritual transformation in the Damascus Road experience opened him to understand the complexity of being a Christian in a multicultural, more open environment. **Paul** faced challenges far beyond **Saul's** Pharisaic protocols.

God's encounters with Abraham, Isaac, and Jacob spoke of a nation yet to be formed. After the Exodus, Moses' Sinai experience resolved social disorder in the desert. We note three steps in the sequence of God's involvement:

1) God's deliverance: freed slave people.
2) God's revelation: the people need a core identity. Moses' encounter with God calls for faith. God is recognized as sovereign Lord. Israel accepts God's authority and guidelines for its cultural ethos. This will mark the people as God's chosen; then,
3) God's word: his presence as commandments (Exod 20:1-17).

The Hebrew term translated "commandment" in English Bibles simply indicates "word." The "word" reveals God's intention, will, for covenant behavior – with God, with neighbor, with self. Acceptance of the word stimulates a desire to fulfill expectations. We discover this word (Sinai's commandments, Exod 20:1-17) addresses two major needs: 1) honor covenant identity; and 2) correct unright relationships. From this beginning develops Israel's ever-expanding body of Levitical law, the community's way of making the word relevant to particulars in both material and spiritual life.

Commandments 1-3 deal with loyalty to God. The Exodus shows God's saving power is for the community. People should not devise rival loyalties to satisfy private desires. People should not attach the Lord's name/power to their human intentions, e.g., "In the name of God I curse you."

Commandments 4 and 5 identify key social institutions and the loyalty both require. Sabbath rest sustains the priority of covenant, an alternative to self-absorption in self-as-self. Honoring "father and mother" (not just genetic parents, but the range of one's kin-bound relations) is essential for people without territorial roots ... common in early Eastern cultures. Members honor the collective of family connections. These sets of relationships are dynamic and form character, allegiance, loyalty – one's heritage. It is the bonding substance for interdependent relationships, the foundation for healthy continuity.

Commandments 6-10 are familiar *"shalt not"* behaviors. These identify social and interpersonal ills familiar from Israel's history and memory – long before enslavement in Egypt. These are wrongs that cause social deterioration for the third and fourth generations.

Sinai's word forms a covenant people from the unwieldy band of wandering ex-slaves. It is for here-and-now. It is about their life and death ... and life beyond death.

After some centuries John tells of another encounter of Word with people (John 1:14, 17): *And the Word [God's intention] became flesh, and lived among us, and we have seen his glory, the glory as of a father's only son, full of grace and truth...The law indeed was given through Moses, grace and truth came through Jesus Christ.*

Here we have a clear distinction between "old" word and "new" word – word as regulating law and the word as encounter with grace and truth, the word rigidly fixing community behaviors and the word offering transformation.

In the Philippians passage above, Paul identifies Jesus' role as "slave." Some use of the term implies bonded servitude. More generally, the English term "slave/servant" in New Testament literature simply identifies members in a functional household.

Jesus commonly uses the unique slave/servant role to identify relationships. The covenant server is more aptly designated "steward." This indicates a close and highly valued connection of master and server. The good steward never presumes a status of equality with the master. The distinctive mark: the steward knows the master's intention, will, goal, expectation. The master: 1) shares this with the loyal server; and 2) undoubtedly assures it happens in the life/workings of the estate. The master turns over more and more responsibility to the server, and the master (always present in spirit) requires accountability.

The master, in Gospel accounts, takes journeys – both long and brief absences. The server/steward provides food and fiber needed by all in the estate/household. Dues are collected and accounted for; payments are made for debts that arise. Many tasks we label "management" are the steward's ordinary jobs.

55

The key factors in the master-steward relationship are positive and worthy. There is mutual trust. There is mutual understanding – a match of the master's expectations and the steward's capacities. Each has access to the other, it is not a cat-and-mouse hiding game. Most significantly, the goal is clear: to fulfill the master's expectations of rightness.

The steward generally has broad authority: decision-making, hiring and discharging, investment and collection of funds. The authority is a trust. It is knowledge of what is right in terms of the master's character, nature, purpose. The master's work is all things that uphold the master's character. The work of the estate is always the master's. The steward himself does many jobs, including oversight of others' tasks. The master's presence is often "sensed" in the activity of a good and faithful steward.

This brings us to consider the phrase in the Lord's Prayer: "Thy will be done." It is puzzling indeed to think of all that might be encompassed in a subject as unwieldy as God's expectations for earth's 7 billion people! That's not what we have to think about.

The quotations from Paul's letters given above use the words "slave" and "will." It might make it clearer if we consider "server/steward" (for slave) and "work" (for will).

In the previous meditation, we noted new birth in the Spirit. We cited Henry Lyte's hymn version of Psalm 103 and the benefits experienced by those in covenant with God. Each benefit transforms in some way: ransom (from bondages of all descriptions); heal (from all forms of physical and emotional disintegration); restore (to fellowship with God and others); forgive (reconcile to God). This gives an agenda for stewards: to identify, locate, and redeem the lost – lost in space, lost in value, lost in beauty (image of God).

This is the will of God; this is the work of God. This is God's presence as Redeemer. This is "Thy kingdom come."

Jesus is without peer as an exemplar of a good "server" in our world. But it is clearer if we use the concept of steward. God's work, God's purpose for this world is the gathering of the separated, lost, marginalized. God is with us, we are not alone. Those *"transformed by the renewing of your minds"* discern and seek who is lost and who is unloved.

The designation of *"good and faithful servant/steward"* is not a phrase added to an annual performance review of professional church/religious workers. It comes when you are asked *"Do you believe?"* and respond joyfully with appropriate behavior.

Meditation Ten

Catch Your Breath

True to your word, you let me catch my breath and send me in the right direction.   (Psalm 23:3 Peterson)

If any want to become my followers, let them deny themselves and take up their cross and follow me. For those who want to save their life will lose it, and those who lose their life for my sake, and for the sake of the gospel, will save it. For what will it profit them to gain the whole world and forfeit their life? Indeed, what can they give in return for their life?   (Mark 8:34b-37)

Seniors strive to sustain good physical health. Still, we face loneliness, uncertainty, physical decline, after-life doubts. No medication or inoculation prevents these possibilities popping into our consciousness. The antidote is a tryst of our spirit and the Holy Spirit.

Peterson's translation of Psalm 23:3 links with this. The traditional wording reads: *"he restoreth my soul"* (literal translation - *"he gives me back my life"*). "Breath" and "spirit" are the same term in Hebrew. Peterson expresses the idea more dynamically as "catching" one's breath/spirit, inferring one has lost something essential for life. Recovering lost breath restores the capacity for action, for vitality, for living. The psalmist praises God's work in/for us. The one recovering lost breath heads in right directions, ways ... the action of God affects the receiver's personal action.

Teilhard de Chardin shares an insight related to the psalmist's image: *"We are not human beings having a spiritual experience, we are spiritual beings having a human experience."* (In another place, de Chardin states it this way: *"You are not a human being having a spiritual experience. You are a spiritual being immersed in a human experience."* Both wordings carry impact.)

de Chardin provides a clear paradigm (pattern) for Christ's saving work. It makes "born again" something other than a physiological process. We identify more easily with Paul's message in II Corinthians 5:17: *Anyone who belongs to Christ is a new person. The past is forgotten, everything is new.* (CEV)

The call to be "new" is rooted in prophets' pleas to Israel. Some are bold and direct, like Ezekiel's word from God (Ezek 18:30-32, Peterson): *Israel, I'll judge each of you according to the way you live. So turn around! Turn your backs on your rebellious living so that sin won't drag you down. Clean house...Get a new heart! Get a new spirit! Why would you choose to die, Israel? ... Make a clean break! Live!*

Jeremiah shares a similar call from the Lord, but the language is less agitated and significantly more pastoral (Jer 31:33-34, Peterson): *This is the brand-new covenant that I will make with Israel when the time comes. I will write my law on their hearts! And be their God. And they will be my people. They will no longer go around setting up schools to teach each other about God. They'll know me first-hand...I'll wipe the slate clean for each of them. I'll forget they ever sinned!*

The prophetic promise partners with a prayer the psalmist raises (Ps 51:10):

Create in me a clean heart, O God,
and put a new and right spirit within me

The explorations of faith, love, and hope are guided and impelled by religious knowledge, experience. Experience brings us fresher insights and interpretations of God's initiatives. We more clearly discern our identity as spiritual beings engaged in this human experience. It is good to accept this identity with grace and joy rather than shudder in bewilderment like Nicodemus. Let's relate this to particular New Testament figures, each prominent in a familiar parable.

First, we look at "The Good Samaritan" (Luke 10:25ff). Jesus uses this story to help the Jewish religious law scholar define the commandment term "neighbor." The characters in the parable are: a traveler (probably a merchant on the road between Jerusalem and Jericho); thieves; a Levite and a Priest (Jewish temple officials); a Samaritan (an ethnic group not in fellowship with Jews); an innkeeper.

The traveler, overtaken by thieves in a remote section of the road, is beaten, robbed, and left to fend for himself – or die. The Levite appears and avoids involvement; he acts on "rightness" shaped by Levitical law for temple purity. The Priest appears and replicates the Levite's behavior. The Samaritan stops, deals with the injuries, and takes the person to an inn to convalesce. The innkeeper receives the wounded man and agrees to provide support/care until the man is healed enough to move on. The Samaritan assures the innkeeper that all costs will be met on a return visit. Loving initiatives shape the Samaritan's "rightness," not religious approval.

Jesus asks the scholar to identify which of the persons in the story is a neighbor. He replies: *"The one who showed mercy."* It is interesting the scholar's reply does not focus on prescribed obligation, but right initiative.

Let's also consider how the beaten traveler might deal with the Samaritan's initiative. Although it is not mentioned, perhaps there is an unrecorded outcome: a change of heart in the person rescued. The Samaritan's witness/action might cause the beaten traveler to *"catch his breath,"* experience a new spiritual identity. We might even say he meets future human experiences as a new, spiritual being.

Next, we consider "The Prodigal Son," often relabeled "The Forgiving Father" (Luke 15:11ff). We consider only two figures: the father and the younger son who takes his share of the estate and leaves the family.

This son chooses to detach himself from family bonding – independence seems more fulfilling than interdependence. His behavior before departure verges on the beastly – self overriding other considerations. The father's character features grace and generosity. The son goes away and lives out his societal fancies but ends up in social isolation – living as one among farm beasts … lost. Luke writes (15:17): "*…when he [the son] came to himself…*" he evaluates benefits of family bonding/belonging. We sense a fresh Spirit moves him to "*catch his breath*," remember the rightness of home. He is found; it is a redemptive moment. What a change – self becomes a spiritual being.

The injured, deserted traveler and the self-imploding younger son both encounter radical inner re-creation: a new heart. That gift is more than a new feeling; the energy of spiritual initiative reforms the lost.

Few of us are born with a passkey to eternal life and presented a halo as assurance. Most of us recognize unrightness in character or behavior. But no senior who calls Jesus Lord ever disqualifies as a spiritual being … even while sharing this fragile human experience.

The intention of these **Meditations** is recovery of spiritual freshness as adult vigor fades, becomes drab, weakens. Hold close the faith promise that touched the psalmist's life and continues for each of us: "*who satisfies you with good as long as you live so that your youth is renewed like the eagle's.*" (Psalm 103:5) The promise is not that we become a fledgling eaglet weakly calling for attention in a lonely, lofty aerie. The promise: God sustains life in our maturity, and death shall have no dominion over that life.

We explore God and encounter God's features. In my own experience I am overwhelmed by the glorious benefits I grasp – if only in part. My exploration of myself as a spiritual being never lessens but it does change – always with greater clarity. Grace has an amazing capacity to make me see how God's right continually transforms any human and cultural descriptions of right.

The communion of saints, the collective of spiritual beings, has a long alumni list. And how interesting we can presume that dear Nicodemus, so hesitant when he came in the night to Jesus, did "*catch his breath*" and became a spiritual being, "*born again.*" In John 19:39, it is written that Nicodemus joined Joseph of Arimathea to prepare Jesus' body for burial in the garden tomb. He was there to experience Resurrection and Life.

Meditation Eleven

Seek!

Jesus prays –
The goal is for all of them to become one heart and mind –
just as you, Father, are in me and I in you....
so they'll be unified and together as we are –
I in them and you in me....
I have made your very being known to them...
so that your love for me
might be in them
exactly as I am in them.

(John 17:21a, 23a, 26b,c)

The imperative "seek" appears frequently in biblical narratives. Often it carries a note of urgency: Do it now while circumstances are right (Is 55:3):

> *Seek the Lord while he may be found,*
> *call upon him while he is near.*

Sometimes it is an alert or alarm that a present way or undertaking is not right or misses the desired goal (Matt 6:25, 33):

> *...do not worry about your life, what you will eat or what*
> *you will drink...your heavenly Father knows that you need*
> *all these things. But strive first for the kingdom of God...*

Sometimes it assures the spiritual being a desired outcome happens even when it is not clear at present (Matt 7:8):

> *Ask and it will be given you, search, and you will find; knock*
> *and the door will be opened for you.*

If you know your life is *in Christ,* then focus on things that belong to that life (Colossians 3:1):

> *So if you have been raised with Christ, seek the things that*
> *are above, where Christ is...*

Seek! It is an imperative. It marks a time for decision. It has the vibrancy of action, the impetus to strive! It wakens and stirs initiatives. This makes clearer the value and beauty of faithful stewardship.

An exhilarating New Testament illustration is the parable of the lost sheep (Luke 15:13ff). A shepherd is hired to tend 100 sheep grazing on hillsides. One is missing; he must act. A "flock" keeps itself together as a herd when it is not disturbed. So, the shepherd begins to move up rises and down gullies. The missing one is found and reunited with the 99; there is joy and rejoicing. A thread of "restoring completeness" runs through the account: the quality of holy, rightness of all elements together. It may be a sheep, or a coin whose loss alters the loveliness of a necklace, or an irreplaceable child gone away.

This all points to an essential quality impelling our exploration: wholeness. To be whole and complete is to be holy. It includes having health in body and soul. It is the completeness Jesus speaks of in John 17.

The next two **Meditations** prepare us for our three specific explorations. First, consider the origin of the English word "explore."

It comes from the Latin verb *plorare*, literally "to cry out." It is the ancient jargon for hunting wild game (originally for food, only later for sport). Hunters send "criers" (or "beaters") into the bush or forest to shout and beat drums. The noise rouses hidden game and drives animals toward waiting hunters.

Our explorations aim "to bring out of hiding" (rouse) thoughts and queries of spiritual import. It is personal; it is probing. The quarry is the dove of peace and the lamb of redemption. The exploration helps us in many ways:

- Recall spiritual truths glossed over in the press of secular demands.
- Rid spiritual clutter, especially barriers to interdependence.
- Ripen newly forming and partially opened buds of faith.
- Resolve conflicting loyalties.
- Refine possibilities to become assurances.
- Revise our child-of-God resume: less emphasis on achievements and greater scope for grace.

The exploration is vigorous – stretching our less flexible comfort zones. Arrange to be purposefully quiet … in a protected haven for meditation. (Just as Jesus regularly took himself apart for reflection and communion/communication with the Father.) It leads to your tryst with God – a sacramental encounter, a communion transaction.

Our spiritual exploration confirms that personal earth time advances to an end that is a beginning. We will be ready for its newness, its differentness. Ripened faith is a seed-bearing bloom – so no need for gloom. Ripened faith deals with major life changes – always trusting the glory of grace. Grace is not frail, nor restrained by red tape and institutional policies. It means your relationship with God can generate new beginnings, find glory in new ways.

This bonding is sacramental, it is interactive. Faith fosters a new environment – uniquely *green* and a healthy habitat for love. Love is an initiative – offered, received. Love never ends once you possess it and it possesses you. Once you have this love, you live it! It energizes hope.

Hope – and life beyond death – is an expectation often not measured by specific elements. But the expectation is there. Consider the words in this hymn:

Spirit of God, descend upon my heart;
wean it from earth; through all its pulses move;
stoop to my weakness, mighty as Thou art,
and make me love Thee as I ought to love.

I ask no dream, no prophet ecstasies,
no sudden rending of the veil of clay,
no angel visitant, no opening skies;
but take the dimness of my soul away.

Hast Thou not bid us love Thee, God and King?
All, all Thine own - soul, heart, and strength and mind;
I see Thy cross - there teach my heart to cling;
O let me seek Thee, and O let me find!

Teach me to feel that Thou are always nigh;
teach me the struggles of the soul to bear,
to check the rising doubt, the rebel sigh;
teach me the patience of unanswered prayer.

Teach me to love Thee as Thine angels love,
one holy passion filling all my frame;
the baptism of the heaven-descending Dove,
my heart an altar and Thy love the flame.

Each of us is a spiritual being – ever engaged in being perfected. It is the quest for being holy, whole. Jesus says this in the Sermon on the Mount (Matt 6:22): *The eye is the lamp of the body. So, if your eye is healthy, your whole body will be full of light.* If we are open and filled with what is right, our lives will be healthy, sound.

In our human experience we collect "trophies" that recognize our contribution in life's shared experience. So I appreciate the recognition but never identify it as signs of my perfection. Seniors in our congregation in

India (as well as other seniors) shared this approach to human recognitions and aging. It is from Hindu sacred writings.

> *You have a right to perform your prescribed duty/action, but*
> *you are not entitled to their fruits. Never claim self as the*
> *cause of your achievements, and never allow yourself to fail*
> *to fulfill your duty.*   (Bhagavad Gita 2:47)

I am a new creation *in Christ.* It's a new life, a new spirit, a new soul … from an old cross that ransoms, heals, restores, forgives.

> *So I'll cherish the old rugged cross, till my trophies at last I lay down;*
> *I will cling to the old rugged cross, and exchange it some day for a crown.*

The senior years are often referred to as life's evening time. Our culture considers "evening" as the end of the day. Evening is when we leave our daily labors and prepare for sleep – renewal for the coming round of work! Hebrew culture reckons evening/night renewal begins the day. The evening hour celebrates grace. One enjoys refreshment with dear ones; engages in rest and restoration. Then comes morning – refreshed, we engage in earthly duties.

A prayerful evening hymn draws on references to Mark 1:32ff, Mark 2:32-34; Luke 5:17ff). The writer Henry Twells celebrates eventide grace:

> *At even, when the sun was set, the sick, O Lord, around Thee lay;*
> *O in what divers pains they met! O with what joy they went away!*

> *Once more 'tis eventide, and we, oppressed with various ills, draw near:*
> *What if Thy form we cannot see? We know and feel that Thou art here.*

> *O Savior Christ, our woes dispel: for some are sick, and some are sad,*
> *and some have never loved Thee well, and some have lost the love they had.*

> *O Savior Christ, Thou too art man; Thou hast been troubled, tempted, tried;*
> *Thy kind but searching glance can scan the very wounds that shame would hide.*

Thy touch has still its ancient power; no word from Thee can fruitless fall:
Hear in this solemn evening hour, and in Thy mercy heal us all.

So, blessed with rest and grace prepare to explore.

Meditation Twelve

Ready – Get Set

...another follower of Jesus said, "Master, excuse me for a couple of days, please. I have my father's funeral to take care of." Jesus refused, "First things first. Your business is life, not death. Follow me. Pursue life."

Passing along, Jesus saw a man at his work collecting taxes. His name was Matthew. Jesus said, "Come along with me." Matthew stood up and followed him.

(Matthew 8:21-22; 9:9, Peterson)

"Soul" identifies a nonbiological part of us humans. It is the energy/spirit that impels or deters action, decision. For a Christian, it identifies awareness of spiritual encounter. The soul sustains values – measures of rightness. Values sustain personal discretion, preferences about what is important. The soul sustains compatibility beyond the self: rightness in others, rightness of God. Right values are a spiritual immune system, antiviral protectors and guardians of inner health. Values 1) keep actions right and reasonable, and 2) shape goals so decisions lead to peace, *shalom*.

Our human experience is a blend of biology (life science) and biography (life story). Biology deals with chemistry and mechanisms that generate and sustain a self's life. It involves genetic initiatives that change with maturing and aging. It involves awareness and unawareness of choices we make to care for the self.

Humans also engage in relationships – self relating to other selves. There seems to be a subconscious drive for this, but it is also a self-conscious quality beyond instinct. The story of our self-conscious initiatives shapes our biography. It is the causes and patterns of how each acts and interacts. Biology and biography blend in our human experience to waken pride, regret, elation, grief, sense of satisfaction, lack of fulfillment.

Value in nature is both practical (for interdependency, e.g., the food-chain) and aesthetic (parts rightly proportioned, i.e., pleasing, in harmony). Values deal with more than facts. They accommodate mystery, enchantment, peace, *shalom*. The soul alerts us to what is unright and why. Unrightness is spiritual when it damages relationships. That damage, generically, is sin – any barrier between self and a healing remedy.

John 1:14, 16 confirms a remedy: *And the Word became flesh and lived among us, and we have seen his glory…full of grace and truth…From his fullness we have all received grace upon grace.* "Fullness" indicates no part is missing – that generates contentment. Its more hidden meaning is a state of inner serenity, *shalom*. John notes that *from his fullness we have all received grace upon grace.*

Grace provides what endures, continues unchanged (in life and in life beyond death). Paul says this grace blesses us with the values that *"abide"* – faith, love, hope (I Cor 13:13). These are soul-size values – right energy to perfect our human experience, a channel for spiritual energy to bless our human experience.

The passages from Matthew cited above are about Jesus' encounter with two persons. Both positively respond with a desire to "follow." ("Follow" is more than trailing along behind Jesus; it indicates a desire for bonding, a readiness for fresh input in one's biography.)

Then suddenly comes the issue of <u>readiness</u>! One wants a two-day leave to bury his father – a very human engagement. The other, Matthew, immediately leaves his civil service appointment as tax collector (considered a sinful occupation by Jews) and follows. We confront the urgency of the imperative: "Follow!" "Come!."

Preceding **Meditations** considered memories and forgotten fragments in our faith experience. It bears century-old marks (and scars) of human experience. But for a senior, it is very personal, more urgent. It is a present-time invitation to be complete as a spiritual being. A person brings all – warts and whatever – face-to-face with grace. What's so impelling? A readiness for wholeness and desire for continuity.

The coming explorations retrace God's initiatives happening **in** but not **of** (i.e., native to) this particular natural world. It reveals *divine* and *human* are compatible but not identical. Covenant connects them, it is both/and rather than either/or: visible/invisible, outer/inner, temporal/otherworldly, existential/eternal.

We refresh ownership of God's covenant benefits: wellness and wholeness. Each comes *"Just as I am."* Each finds good news' blessing for real heart hungers. The explorations engage us more concertedly to *"Hear the Word of God."* I do it more maturely *and* more childlike. I see how matured spirit impacts character. *In Christ* I am more of a saint than ever. I give myself permission to bear God's holiness. I identify myself as a spiritual being. It is not a pious pose; it doesn't program me in strange posturing.

A positive response brings new ownership. It is like Mary's response to the Holy Spirit at the annunciation: *"Will you bear [carry] God's holiness?"* (Mary's response, *"Here am I, your servant,"* completes the exchange.) God's verbs (actions) now become my verbs, God's love shapes my love. I de-mythologize any arbitrary and rigid divide of secular and holy. I stop filtering the spiritual through a dark and spooky glass. I react less to conditions and act more by God's grace. The sides of the coin are no longer sin/purity (competitive concepts) but forgiven/made whole (complementary initiatives). It's the gist of the old chorus:

Thank you, Lord, for saving my soul,
Thank you, Lord, for making me whole,
Thank you, Lord, for giving to me,
Thy great salvation so rich and free.

God is proactive, God comes – the Incarnation. The creator re-creates closeness with the creature who remains uniquely in his image. Now is the right time for spiritual exploration. Our mind-set may be shadowed by feelings of inadequacy, isolation, worry. Still, it is the right time. It is the <u>now</u> moment Dante claims in the opening lines of "Inferno" in *The Divine Comedy*:

Midway in the journey of our life
I came to myself in a dark wood,
For the straight [i.e. direct] way was lost.

A heart-touching aptness of this "right time" is the theme for a song about two persons in love, who defer a commitment to marriage. Each is too wrapped up in "self"; each carries on life in his/her own "boat." One cannot settle – establish a ground for continuity. The other cannot chance exploration – unfurl sails and catch wind for awaiting horizons and experience. We listen to this soulful refrain:

Your little boat has no anchor
and my little boat has no sail!

Spiritual exploration involves unpledging allegiance to anything that hinders/fears God's new beginnings and abundant fulfillment. It requires hoisting a protective anchor and allowing God's initiatives to fill sails. It is not easy – especially in life's senior season. The saving assurance is a bonding of covenant trust. Prepare to encounter the One who makes all things new.

The Christian's life beyond death is yet to be revealed. It is the consummation of a covenant promise. The promise is not what you *acquire* but what you *become*. And this opens a new perspective of our place and part in "glory." It is about being with God and God being with us. Seniors sensing inner deadness should anticipate rebirth. It's a deep-inside cry, marking an end of spiritual hibernation. Christopher Fry expresses this rightness in his drama *A Sleep of Prisoners*:

Dark and cold we may be, but this
Is no winter now. The frozen misery
Of centuries breaks, cracks, begins to move.
The thunder is the thunder of the floes,
The thaw, the flood, the upstart Spring.
Thank God our time is now when wrong
Comes up to face us everywhere,
Never to leave us till we take
The longest stride of soul men ever took.
Affairs are now soul size.
The enterprise
Is exploration into God.

The enterprise is a venture, an endeavor. It is not a study about God. It is an exploration into God who opens himself to us.

Affairs Are Now Soul Size

Do not let the grace of God go for nothing…see, now is the acceptable time, now is the day of salvation.

(II Corinthians 6:1b,2b)

The Great Depression and World War II imposed stressful economic limitations ... but not on my childhood anticipation of Christmas Day at home! Gifts and food were carefully garnered; generational bonding was abundant. How true the hymn! *"Blest be the tie that binds."*

Charles Dickens' *A Christmas Carol* (1843) dramatizes the importance of bonding, human ties – blessing known, blessing recovered. Jacob Marley (Scrooge's deceased partner) kept to himself what he valued (his wealth). In death, he carries a haunting burden of his unright, earthly stewardship. He drifts eternally: not at rest, not connected, not missed. At Christmastime, Marley shares his sad outcome with Scrooge; it is a *life beyond death* Scrooge can still avoid. Scrooge heeds Marley's warning about what one loses by <u>un</u>right living.

Charles Wesley's Christmas hymn (1744) anticipates another kind of personal, spiritual encounter:

> *Come, thou long-expected Jesus, born to set your people free;*
> *from our fears and sins release us, let us find our rest in thee.*

Our <u>fears</u> (*phobos*): what terrifies us, makes us apprehensive – our vulnerabilities, our defenses, our insecurities. They encase our spirits as a stifling armor. Still we fail to deflect the long-term effects of fears within, fears without.

Our <u>sins</u> (*amartia*): errors, offenses, hurtful propensities, unright actions – our wrong inclinations and initiatives. We endorse what divides; we foster competitive, isolating behaviors. Tranquillity eludes us. God's call in Eden persists: *"Adam [person, child] where is my created and chosen?"*

Jesus offers solace. *"Come unto me, all you that are weary and are carrying heavy burdens, and I will give you rest."* (Matt 11:28). It is enticing and relevant. Christ's peace *frees* us, his holy peace transforms our **un**rest. His peace resolves the clashing dissonance of earth noise around us/within us! The peace is both capacity and energy for spirit transformation. Planet Earth massed into form ages ago, silently turning in the dark – unnoticed, lifeless. Then something groped its way through the blackness, found Earth's face, stayed and played upon it. The light had come! Christ is light – energy redeeming failed attempts and trivial tries, light as healing and assuaging grace. The light brings a new way, a new life. You'll know it if you enter it ... or, if you don't!

With light comes health and wholeness: color, beauty, and life itself. God's glory that once shone through space's darkness comes to our darkness, our unrightness, our clutch of terrors. The difference between a mass of dark, dead matter spinning, and this earth touched with redeeming creativity – that's the difference Christ makes for those bonded with him. Christ's light touches and makes right dark loyalties.

In Shakespeare's *Henry VIII*, Cardinal Wolsey's schemes distort his sense of right before God and his integrity and stewardship as Lord Chancellor of England. Eventually, it destroyed his bond of loyalty with the King. The Cardinal accuses no one but himself. Wolsey laments to his colleague Cromwell:

> *O Cromwell, Cromwell!*
> *Had I but served my God with half the zeal*
> *I served my king, he would not in mine age*
> *Have left me naked to mine enemies.*

Any encounter with Christ resets how we measure values; never again is some childish "make do" sufficient. Picture this scene: a boy is told to wash his hands before dinner; he returns, shows his hands, and coyly comments: *"They're not clean, but at least they match!"* (A childish ploy to excuse half-heartedness.)

It is difficult to shake off behaviors and attitudes that keep our wholeness vulnerable. Habits are comfortable. Christ offers energy for a new inner order: grace. Grace reaches a deep, non-biodegradable part of me!

God's final word to your life and mine isn't about everlasting demands; it's about everlasting arms! This *"maker of heaven and earth"* wants to say simply that he fashions you, and you can count on him not to forget it. He isn't going to give life to a human soul then leave it without any further pains on his part to get along as best it can!

Seniors sensing inner deadness should anticipate rebirth. Each must decide how to respond to this call. Do you react defensively or find blessing in waiting, eternal arms? Rest in those arms clears a way to experience the offer of the manger, and the cross and the empty tomb, and Pentecost. The *chrysalis* time is over. Break out from that shrink-wrap, airless casing of fear and sin! In that release God wakens a hibernating part of us! Affairs are <u>now</u> soul size!

This new alertness is more about *open up* than *clean up*! Accept revelation. God wants you to trust how he values you. God wants you to accept his invitation for partnership: be a steward of grace in the real world. It is a full-blown gift, freely given – an expression of love in action.

The awaiting exploration into God connects with holy mystery, holy power. It is grace-full fellowship. We know its risk. We expose ourselves to spiritual connection, communion. We allow ourselves to be found, known. We own Bernard of Clairvaux's affirmation:

> *Jesus, the very thought of thee with sweetness fills the breast;*
> *but sweeter far thy face to see, and in thy presence rest.*

The Bible's narrative persists with a single theme: amid amazing earth achievements, a human being is still lost. Let's not trivialize this! High and low, young and old, comfortable and poor, Pharisee and publican, male and female, first world and third world – our feet may seem on solid ground, but only *in Christ* are we found. The only distinction is between the few who know it and the many who do not. Now it is a coin, now a sheep, sometimes a child – but the most immutable value of each lies in the redeeming love that
- feels about, searching in the dark nooks and crannies, or
- sets itself through the night, with an eerie shepherd's call, into the steep ravine, or
- waits forever and a day by the gate, yonder where the road runs in from thousands of far countries!

Persons caught up in great suffering often ask a pastor or a friend: *"Why does this happen to me?"* I have no words as an answer for that, only an expectation. Now is a daybreak of opportunity: *"From our fears and sins release us, let us **find** our rest **IN** thee."*

Our senior spiritual exploration moves us into light. The enterprise moves beyond the constructs of logic to mystery. The Creator's gift now is closer than ever expected. The Light happens! Live in it! There are answers we have to <u>live out</u>, not <u>spell out</u>. This is a first-person affair. Each recognizes:

> *Affairs are now soul size.*
> *The enterprise*
> *Is exploration into God.*

Faith

The earth's environment abounds in natural beauty and grandeur: sunsets, tree-edged lake shorelines, rugged mountain ranges, wondrous geological formations. The hymn *How Great Thou Art* praises God's initiatives in creation. These sense experiences move us to lyric praise. Psalm 19:1-7a (Peterson) is a dramatic human response:

God's glory is on tour in the skies, God-craft on exhibit across the horizon.
Madame Day holds classes every morning, Professor Night lectures each evening.
Their words aren't heard, their voices aren't recorded,
But their silence fills the earth: Unspoken truth is spoken everywhere.
God makes a huge dome for the sun – a superdome!
The morning sun's a new husband leaping from his honeymoon bed,
The day-breaking sun an athlete racing to the tape.
That's how God's Word vaults across the skies from sunrise to sunset,
Melting ice, scorching deserts, warming hearts to faith.
The revelation of God is whole and pulls our lives together.

We experience this physical world as visible "glory." The experience is also spiritual – a reminder human completeness involves something outside ourselves. So we explore faith.

Faith is an exchange, a transaction between God and self. Paul expresses it one way: The old Adam is now the new Adam in Christ. (I Cor 15:22). This exchange bonds us with the Lord and resets the measure of right in us. It's the transition of human being to spiritual being. Faith engages me: I accept God's initiatives and recognize their blessings in/for me. It answers Jesus' haunting questions (Mark 8:36-7): *"For what will it profit [persons] to gain the whole world and forfeit their life? Indeed, what can they give in return for their life?"* This gives faith a distinguishing quality: It is *living* faith.

Eugene Peterson catches the dynamic in this exchange (Romans 5:1-4):

By entering through faith into what God has always wanted to
do for us – set us right with him, make us fit for him – we have
it all together with God because of our Master Jesus. And that's
not all! We throw open our doors to God and discover at the
same moment that he has already thrown open his door to us
[i.e., covenant bonding]. *We find ourselves standing where we*

78

always hoped we might stand – out in the wide open spaces of
God's grace and glory, standing tall and shouting with praise.

The familiar phrase *"justified by faith"* now has benefits and power. Paul specifies faith as the way we seal (confirm) this transition. It is something to live and share, not reserve for discussion and debate. Faith prompts a response from deep within, like Psalm 103:1: *"Bless the Lord, O my soul, and* **all** *that is within me, bless his holy name."*

William Gaither echoes this in his gospel hymn: *"Something happened, and now I know, [the Lord] touched me and made me whole."*

Faith-bonding roots in Hebrew tradition. Isaiah 26:3 speaks of this covenant blessing (CEV translation): *"The Lord gives perfect peace to those whose faith is firm."* Additionally, God's revelations and initiatives anticipate our response.

Let's consider two uses of "tree" in the Bible – *vis-à-vis* the human response, i.e., faith. (The tree image is both real and symbolic, literal, and an image.)

In Eden, God plants a tree of the knowledge of good and evil (Gen 2:17). The tree is God's standard; it identifies the creator's rightness. "Good" indicates what is right for health (wholeness). "Evil" is anything that erodes and corrupts right. It is more than an ethical reminder; it indicates the Lord's presence. It is tinged with mystery. It validates life qualities: be holy, whole, healthy. Centuries later Israel receives some specific duties to measure right in its common life – the Law.

The second tree is man-made, hoisted on Calvary. Authorities (religious and civil in concert) used it for the death of Jesus. The death is a human judgment rejecting Jesus' way, right, claims. The ensuing resurrection is a divine judgment affirming God's intention for rightness, life renewed.

The tree in both instances links to God's covenant initiative. It sets rightness outside human measures. In the cross "for-the-time-being" encounters the eternal; that tree intensifies God's intentions and God's call to covenant faith. My response impels my transition to a spiritual being.

Isaiah prophesied a heavenly Messiah entering our space, in future time. The birth of Jesus is anticipation happening. God is with us, Emmanuel. Faith once thought personal conviction is now the dynamic that shapes personal lifestyle.

Faith is an exchange from death to life: God's initiatives possess me, my acceptance of these is faith. It is the spiritual maturity Paul lauds in I Cor 2:9,10,12 (v. 9 cites Isaiah 64:4 & 65:17):

> *What no eye has seen, nor ear heard,*
> *nor the human heart conceived,*
> *what God has prepared for those who love him –*
> *these things God has revealed to us through the Spirit; for the Spirit*
> *searches everything, even the depths of God…now we have*
> *received not the spirit of the world, but the Spirit that is from God,*
> *so that we might understand the gifts bestowed on us by God.*

Jesus intends his character to be the disciples' character: *followership.* Followership is disciples' lifestyle, not passive presence in an entourage. (Dietrich Bonhoeffer describes this lifestyle as "the cost of discipleship"). Followers welcome, own, and witness the Master's initiatives and accept a new identity: steward – s/he acts in the name of the Lord!

The steward's followership is a matter neither of pride nor shame; it is the nature of a spiritual being. It opens human experience to redemptive options. Paul's personal exploration brought him this insight: *"For I am not ashamed of the gospel, it is the power of God for salvation to everyone who has faith."* (Rom 1:16). Paul's followership moment comes on the Damascus Road. It is divine initiative; the risen Lord (now as the Holy Spirit) comes to Paul. The exchange reveals a world vision to Paul.

Earlier we noted values. Paul notes three abiding Christian virtues: faith, love, hope. These marks of excellence assess both common morality and personal behavior. These virtues identify those *in Christ.* The virtues then come alive through the steward's initiatives.

So our senior exploration begins with meditations on God's revelation of himself: actions revealing his nature. In the beginning God creates – apart from human experience. In the fullness (ripeness) of time, we encounter God as redeemer and sustainer … as part of our human experience. The redeemer – Jesus – embodies rightness and beauty (right relationships) in this human experience. The sustainer – Holy Spirit – ripens beauty and glory in faithful stewards.

Exploration I is a threefold progression: God-with-us as 1) Son, 2) Holy Spirit, 3) self *in Christ*. Our senior concern is the latter – life as a steward, as expressed in Colossians 1:26-27 (Peterson):

> *This mystery has been kept in the dark for a long time, but now it is out in the open. God wanted everyone, not just Jews, to know this rich and glorious secret inside and out, regardless of their background, regardless of their religious standing. The mystery in a nutshell is just this: Christ is in you, so therefore you can look forward to sharing in God's glory.*

Meditations Fourteen – Nineteen deal with God's self-revelation ... the full progression of Jesus taking the form of a human being to his return to fullness as a spiritual being. Our response to this revelation delineates the joy of our faith – contentment of self *in Christ*.

Jesus' birth happens in an earthly context: a baby in a manger,
in a stable, in a village.
People come with whetted expectations – personal, and shared.
It's more "Let's go and see!" than "We've come – now what?"
The encounter is not a solution; it initiates a revelation.
Does the visit awaken faith? Do behaviors change?
(A baby is born, but nothing seems to be far-reaching in it all.
Visitors come in haste, then depart – back to the old routines.
Maybe something more will happen. Meanwhile perhaps it's best to get
back to normal – pay the bills and raise the family!)
The new journey is not about *words* we live with,
but a new initiative – the *Word* living in us.

A Human Being, Full of Grace and Truth

The Word became a human being, full of grace and truth, and lived among us.
(John 1:14)
I believe in one Lord Jesus Christ...who for us men and for our salvation came down from heaven, and was incarnate by the Holy Spirit of the Virgin Mary.
(The Nicene Creed)

We carry on doing "same old, same old," then it's Christmas! God himself disrupts ordinary living! God's purposes and intentions live in a human. In Jesus' ministry, we discover how God's initiative tailors precisely for every "now" in a person's human journey. (It's called good news!) It's an exchange: bonding brings benefits. God offers life that echoes the creator's intention at Eden – now lost in nonending cultural mutations. Fullness awaits – a better option than the *status quo*.

John 1:14 claims Jesus represents the offer: *The Word became a human being ... and lived among us.* We sense *"a human being ... among us"* is like a neighbor, in our time and space. Such a presence is approachable, flesh and blood.

John 1:12-13 affirms it's a transforming offer: *... to all who did receive him, to those who have yielded him their allegiance, he gave the right to become children of God ... the offspring of God himself.* God's offer is personal and universal; all can take <u>ownership</u> of new and everlasting life. Do I recognize its profound relevance for me with the conditions and characters in Bethlehem's drama? (There's a place for everyone in it all!)

<u>Mary and Joseph</u>. Mary is a teenager betrothed to Joseph. A divine visitor brings her news: God chooses you to bear Jesus, a king in the line of David. He will hold the title "Son of God" (Luke 1:35).

What happens to Mary happens to us when we let Christmas be personal. The Holy Spirit chooses us to receive and bear God's holiness in our lives. Our response indicates a new identity and wakens faith.

Although puzzled, Joseph accepts his marriage/parental role so Jesus knows a family setting. Family is the core social relationship in which self is discovered, develops, wrestles to find integrity. Family assures healthy belonging. It's where one learns and trusts connection and interdependence. Birth is part of biological life; family is part of covenant-life.

Mary and Joseph accept God's call to be stewards of grace.

<u>Bethlehem</u>. Joseph's native (hereditary) village is Bethlehem. The place identifies beginnings, natural community, an album where our face belongs. It is biological and biographical continuity. One's space in this world is important, it fosters security.

<u>The Stable</u>. Bethlehem's inn is full. Crowds jostle – everyone is on the move. Birth is imminent; Joseph and Mary adapt. God engages us when/where we least expect it – and later discover the time/place was right! Jesus' birth space is a cattle stall. (A setting much like our lives: foul, soiled –

seldom spruced up, neat, prepared.) God becomes part of life-on-the-move, more than arranges a theatrical welcome.

Baby. The Lord begins life among us as a baby. This is significant. A baby in a family changes everything. There is a new center in the home. So the Word meets us with arms outstretched, dependent on our responses.

Beasts. These are tethered animals, kept to bear burdens, objects of human impatience. Later such a beast bears "king" Jesus entering Jerusalem, *en route* to death on a thief's cross, bearing our transgression. (*Surely he has known our grief.* Isaiah 52-53)

Angels. Heaven's song wafts earthward – over rural hillsides. If people want to hear this song, they must look up (outside eye-level circles of concern)!

Noise fills Bethlehem – people complaining, displaced, and impatient. The angels' song could not be heard in that context. *Otherworldly* messages rarely halt traffic. Life fills with sounds of human enterprise – car horns, cash machines, electronic signals alerting us to urgent updates en route to our next destination. Only in a silent space will we get a message from beyond our multitasking environments. An angel's call to joy and peace isn't recorded!

Shepherds. These simple folk heed signals and demands of life around them. They expect nothing new; out-of-the-ordinary things seldom come to them. Their life span time/space is routine. Angels mention the birth of a baby – news, but not new; the **new** news is a "savior." They listen, they respond.

Shepherd-villagers hear news: a gift of new life for a neighboring family. They hasten to share the information and together visit the newborn. They snatch any token of support at hand: an egg, a piece of cloth. The gesture conveys belonging and bonding – a traditional welcome for one whose life-journey begins, with its own share of hardship and sadness. They go to the manger to see if what was told is really so! Most of us seldom expect messages from above. We settle for overhyped options on TV or by email! Grace freely given is a rarity with our normal suppliers.

Magi. The philosophers, sages, search beyond what is known; they innovate. They master disciplines that probe connections yet-to-be-identified. They like mystery and seek clues to alluring "unknowns," things awaiting discovery. More alert than most, they discern indicators of fuller truth. We jest and say their heads are in the clouds. (It is their nature to look up and respond, i.e., follow. They do look up and often find real clarity, not just mist.)

This event bears marks of radical change. The star is new – not part of observed cycles. Surely it's a sign of an out-of-the-ordinary intention, verity. They follow its lead to the stable, then heed spirit-guidance and take a new route.

<u>The Gathered</u> become one as they circle the manger! Various kinds of excitement and wonder warm the camaraderie in that dimly lit space. (It is a living nativity scene, comfortable for many of us.) Here we see:
- The holy family: humble, devout, obedient, puzzled, joyful.
- The shepherds/villagers: uncomplicated women, men and children, relying on others' integrity and goodwill for contentment and satisfaction.
- The wise: vulnerable, agreeing to open themselves to dimensions of truth outside usual comfort zones!

At the manger they are a body, not categories – unaware of what unites them. They sense this is more than a happenstance event. Leaving the manger, each ponders: What does this encounter mean? Who is this infant? Is this a new beginning, a transition? Will there be further involvement with this person – this Savior, this Christ, this Lord? God does something public, yet personal. How can I know its benefits?

Every celebration of Bethlehem's manger affirms W.H. Auden's insight in his oratorio-poem, *For the Time Being*:

Remembering the stable where for once in our lives
*Everything became a **You** and nothing was an **It**.*

New life implies some alteration. Birth begets new demands and relationships affecting everyone's development. The faith journey begins and ripens. The allure is there; the risk is owning it – followership. The critical factor here is me and my readiness for this kind of faith.

Meditation Fifteen

An *epiphany* is a particular experience/insight.
A true *epiphany* affects the spirit – a less visible dimension.
(The term has a Greek origin – it means "seeing," "clear understanding.")
Epiphany is more than visual sensation. It affects our identity. It is a gift
originating outside oneself, received and acted on.
It is a *Eureka!* event – an awareness that enriches experience.
This **Meditation** is about Simeon's *epiphany*: He perceives
Jesus is the expected Messiah.
Epiphany: an essential part of any covenant encounter.
Our senior *epiphany* extends the particular affirmation "Jesus as Lord,"
to the transforming experience of "seeing" self *in Christ.*

Owning the Gift

"Master, now you are dismissing your servant in peace, according to your word;
for my eyes have seen your salvation, which you have prepared in the presence
of all peoples, a light for revelation to the Gentiles and for glory to your people
Israel."   (Luke 2:29-32)

The day we first arrived in India, Sylvia and I lodged at a Christian guesthouse in an old, crowded part of Mumbai (Bombay). Outside the gate were an elevated main rail line and a busy street market. Our eyes and ears and noses filled with exotic sights and sounds and aromas. As evening turned to night, darkness veiled it all; urban bustle settled into silence.

Our sleep was interrupted with recurring *thuds* – the sound of a sturdy staff striking pavement. *Thud,* followed by a shrill whistle blast, then silence.

At breakfast our hostess chortled when we mentioned this. She said it was the *chowkidar's* (watchman) assuring signals (normal for Indian homes and villages). The thuds and whistles 1) alert intruders that a watchman is present, and 2) assure residents that all is well.

The *chowkidar* has old and honored functions throughout the East: 1) to guard and protect and 2) to report unusual sightings observed in the night skies. Sightings alert residents it is again time for recurring happenings. Religious observations are set by phases of the moon. Sowing and planting begin when certain morning stars reappear on the horizon. The learned (secular and sacred) heed these calls to readiness.

Simeon and Anna – senior Jews at the time of Jesus' birth – did temple service. Earlier, Simeon was assured he would live to see the promised Messiah. Joseph and Mary bring Jesus to the temple for a birth-blessing. Simeon's sighting of the infant is an *epiphany* – a promise realized. Cradling the child, he prays: *"God, now release your servant in peace [shalom] as you promised – with my own eyes I've seen your salvation."* (Simeon's release is from a *chowkidar* role, keeping watch.) His faith is honored. He experiences the realness of God.

A hope is realized. Release bestows *shalom,* spiritual wholeness. Simeon is an *epiphany* model: "see" (encounter) God's closeness. It initiates and reforms a faith-journey.

Faith matures; we leave the earthly press of prime years. I affirm: *"God-is-with-me."* Now, I enjoy hours on the other side of "for the time being" urgencies. Professional achievements lose primacy. Fewer hopes (and realities!) are on hold.

Oneness with the Lord is no longer pious posturing. It's time to <u>know</u> *shalom.* I draw freely from the treasures of grace.

Life as a senior continues, but *epiphany* confirms a new priority: life *in Christ.* Deal with this human experience accordingly. The angels' Christmas chorus signals: *"Glory to God ... peace to all."* It echoes a creation affirmation: *God looked over what he made and said: "It's so good – what I intend!"* Epiphany happens (the dynamic differs from the more passive expression *"have an epiphany"*). The encounter makes personal what it means to be *in Christ.*

- I hold more closely God's measure of **right.** That often challenges popular gauges of expediency, efficiency.
- I choose to **be** right so energy generates right outcomes. I trust God's leading, so <u>resources</u> and <u>opportunities</u> wed more fruitfully. (This is purposeful, not a presumption that resources and opportunities automatically connect rightly).
- I refine **love:** right verbs/actions shape behaviors with new energy and for different purposes.

Expectation is no longer just an agreeable possibility. Faith's tasks (and anxieties) faced in life's morning and high-noon now cradle in senior peace ... a gift of *shalom.*

I am at ease with my evening-of-life self. I permit myself: a) to revel in memories of blessing, b) to cherish inspiration as much as information, c) to glory in my spouse/family – my grandest comfort and energizer.

I am part of a fellowship of redeemed sinners <u>and</u> imperfect saints! I find more stability in ties that bind than membership ID cards.

I use Spirit time to practice scales of rejoicing – music that celebrates faith more as health than therapy!

And I bask in wonder: God creates, God recreates – and nothing in creation is cheated of his oh-so-amazing grace!

My *epiphany* puts busyness in a fresh perspective. I find it permits me to have a little distance, space – outside the stormy "eye" of enervating activism. Enjoy the senior option to step back from existential moments labeled "urgent." It modifies those jagged ups/downs, goods/bads. ("Distance" improves a view of fine art. Don't stand too near the work; the added space helps integrate elements for clearer meaning.)

Many long for, even seek, an *epiphany* – inner acknowledgment of being one-with-Christ. God doesn't withhold it or hide it. The experience comes when faith has childlike readiness to grasp and claim God's initiatives. God never plays "Simon Says" games. When asked, God gives bread not scorpions; fish not snakes (Matt 7:7-10). *Epiphany* – accepting spiritual bonding!

A person's *epiphany* often happens *via* an unheralded relationship with a spiritual mentor who nurtures readiness. I consider my Seminary New Testament professor in this way. Dr. Kooy was insightful; his style of interpreting scripture was clear and relevant. He was accessible; his criticisms were always apt, usually clearing "foggy" thinking. He had a sense of humor. He was a *guru* – patiently prodding students to let the Word speak when we students sought to insist on a meaning not really in the Word. The fullness in God's Word is never lost in particulars; particulars never infer a forced hidden meaning.

During my first year of studies, a classmate asked Dr. Kooy if Jesus' views about an ancient Hebrew social situation were really relevant. Quite calmly, Dr. Kooy repositioned the perspective of "relevance": *"You may be irrelevant and I may be irrelevant, but Jesus Christ is never irrelevant. Study to see what Jesus reveals resolving the given social situation."*

I found Dr. Kooy a special mentor – an *epiphany* agent, a guide of how one loses/finds one's life for Christ's sake. He helped make straight my way to be *in Christ* – an *epiphany* agent for real Spirit-power. After seminary, I went to India. I only met him again two other times ... but I cherished his spirit-gift during more than 50 years of active ministry.

Amid all the demands facing Joseph and Mary at Jesus' birth, they put their precious infant, named Jesus (*savior*), into Simeon's arms for a blessing.

It became Simeon's *epiphany* – an expectation fulfilled; it blessed him with *shalom*.

Paul notes a personal *epiphany* and bonding *in Christ* (Phil 3:7-9).

Yes, all the things I once thought were so important are gone from my life. Compared to the high privilege of knowing Christ Jesus as my Master, firsthand, everything I once thought I had going for me is insignificant ... so that I could embrace Christ and be embraced by him. I didn't want some petty, inferior brand of righteousness ... when I could get the robust kind that comes from trusting Christ – God's righteousness.

Paul's ministry and witness has a watchman's (*chowkidar*) marks. His writing is never to prove proprietary rightness of his experience. Rather, it reveals life *in Christ* as the source of "right" that brings reconciliation within, without.

At the Ascension, Jesus gives a *chowkidar* assignment. Followers are witnesses – his "presence" before/with others. He alerts close followers about an interim period – wait for (expect) an *epiphany* moment of new covenant bonding, sealed by the Holy Spirit – Pentecost. This gives assurance and power, and orients followers for their stewards' tasks.

For 20 centuries, *followership* determines spiritual beings' role as heralds of Emmanuel – God-is-with-us. It happens in cultures worldwide, in thousands of languages, with words and service … always local, always person-to-person, always faith experienced.

Behavior choices – personal, collective – brought many dark times after Eden.
Good Friday is a dark time – dark actions, dark forebodings.
Spiritual exploration often brings dark moments.
Then, light – perhaps requiring awkward behavior changes.
Holy reflection alters the perspective so we see a more abundant life. It might
involve sacrifice, i.e., give up a thing of lesser value for a finer blessing.
This meditation deals with Job – often a confusing faith-history figure.
Job's life alters when he experiences covenant fellowship - himself-with-God.
It changes Job in this life and expectation for life beyond death.
The Creator's rightness brings Job face-to-face with earth-grounded varieties.
Earth-grounded rightness was used to justify Jesus' crucifixion.

Begin at the Conclusion

*I know that my redeemer lives … at the last he will stand upon the earth … and
then I shall see God.* (Job 19:25)
*I know you can do all things, and that your purposes cannot be denied. … I
heard many thoughts about you, now I encounter you; so I leave my old
presumptions, and repent in dust and ashes* (Job 42:2,5-6)
*…a person named Job…was blameless and upright. He was reverent and turned
from evil.* (Job 1:1)

A *New Yorker* cartoon shows adults chatting socially. One says: *"I'm in the market for an easier religion."*

The crucifixion doesn't make religion easier; it cuts away debilitating spiritual encrustation. It recovers covenant celebration like the poignant image in Psalm 23:3 *"… he restores my soul [literally, 'gives me back my life']."*

Covenant fellowship is the core gospel experience: *The Word became flesh and <u>lived among us</u>, and we have <u>seen</u> his glory…* (John 1:14) Israel doesn't see fellowship as part of covenant life. Perhaps this is why Jesus weeps over Jerusalem prior to his Passion: *"If you only recognized this is your time of God's visitation." (Luke 19:41)*

The book of **Job** prophetically anticipates this core experience. Initially, Job's spirituality is self-directed, lacking dynamic closeness with God! Job sees "fellowship" only as future option – after death. Midway into Job's story he declares: *"I know that my redeemer lives … <u>at the last</u> he will stand upon the earth … and <u>then</u> I shall see God."* (Job 19:25) Covenant fellowship is outside Job's earth-time, earth-space.

Woven in Job's story is a motif of *undeserved suffering*. Life seems God-forsaken, God-<u>not</u>-with-us. Job is a here-and-now realist – his three friends even more so! His religion: a life devoted to conscious right action. Covenant fellowship is a deferred benefit – a then-and-there reality. Perhaps it's an effect caused by moral uprightness. Love's redeeming work is seen as a prize for accrued spiritual capital. Such a conviction easily becomes spiritual baggage:

> *Little Jack/Jill Horner sat in a corner, eating his/her Christmas pie;*
> *he/she stuck in his/her thumb, pulled out a plum*
> *And said "What a good boy/girl am I!"*

The premise: I control fellowship; it's the rewards earned with accrued right actions. It misses the part grace plays – my redeemer holds me in fellowship.

Job <u>ends</u> with an encounter: God sweeps away Job's spiritual clutter and shares fellowship. Job has a radical revelation and finds a simpler religion!

> *I know you can do all things, and that your purposes cannot be denied. … I heard many thoughts about you, now I encounter you; so I leave my old presumptions, and repent in dust and ashes.* (42:2,5-6)

Covenant grace reforms self. That turning point – that <u>end</u> – becomes a faith <u>beginning</u>! We sing: *"End of faith as its beginning"*!

Job (and other Wisdom Literature) uses a familiar literary device. Its action is the hero's/speaker's life-change from spiritual darkness to spiritual light. This abounds in **The Psalms**. Consider Psalm 22. It opens with a person lamenting self without God; by the Psalm's end the speaker sheds spiritual baggage and discovers fellowship. Opening despair – *"My God ... why have you forsaken me?"* – leads to *"I will yet trust in God."*

Christian faith does not gloss over the crucifixion. A human body hangs – beholden to power devoid of grace. Calvary's power is fragile and painfully temporal. The empty tomb reveals power imbued with grace.

Job's sufferings are real – just as the cross is real. Job is not content to leave it at that. When some say he is God-forsaken, he protests.

Job's quest – and ours: discovering a missing dimension of covenant. Job sorts through his behavior baggage. He no longer squanders spiritual energy. He doesn't rest belief on moral achievement; he looks beyond self-rightness. Perhaps we might add a new final verse to Job's saga, a new affirmation: *A person named Job thrived in God's communion!*

Job's suffering (his "Lent") changes his goals, not his character. So we return to Job 1:1 and find his character given clearly and succinctly: *... a person named Job ... was blameless and upright. He was reverent and turned from evil.*

Job, like us outside Eden's securities, strives in Earth's complexities.

Simplistically, we conjecture we are God-forsaken, excluded from covenant fellowship. But wait! Look carefully at this self, Job. He is a:

<u>Self-as-human</u> – *blameless:* (KJV = *perfect*), a person fully equipped and competent to interact with God.

<u>Self-in-community</u> – *upright:* just, in healthy relationships, confident to be a member in a body.

<u>Self-in-covenant</u> – *reverent*, chooses godly, not ungodly alternatives.

A person among persons, under God – not sinless, but in God's image. *"I'm in the market for an easier religion."* This mantra is for the self-sufficient and self-absorbed (like Job's adviser friends). These presume God's detachment, presuming God is adrift in time and space!

Place yourself in Jerusalem during Holy Week. Jewish religious priorities collide with Roman civil order. Jesus is the pawn both sides use to justify their respective best-of-all-possible-worlds. The pathos: both civic and religious baggage clutters all pretenses of rightness. All choose **of**-this-world validation. The cross is mutually convenient. Calvary. Darkness. Nature trembles. Humanity forsakes God. Covenant is obscured; holiness is veiled. God endorses neither side. Waiting. God's choice is to reveal himself after the Jewish sabbath, when Golgotha's dust settles.

The third day. A sealed tomb in a garden, guarded. Dawn. Humanity is not God-forsaken. Something better happens in our world. Shroud-cloths cannot imprison a spiritual being. The Lord shares a breakfast of fresh fish beside still waters on the shores of Lake Galilee.

The cross as weakness remeasures the rightness of earth power. It alters old presumptions and validations about *"What a good girl/boy am I!"* It is good news: There are fortresses of the soul where confrontational power cannot reach, only clinging to rightness provides a resolution.

Job held old presumptions about right living. Perhaps he missed a vital turning point ... his "wait" for its benefits took a wrong turn somewhere along the way. Isaiah's promise happens: *"Be comforted. ... the time of waiting is over!"* (Is 40:1a,2b)

Let me tell of two parishioners in New Delhi, India. Each discovers self's personal fortress falls short of real promise; both discover a self newborn by grace and fostered in love. Strength and weakness become measured by blessings and power of God's grace and disciples' loving acts.

1. Raj. August 1947, India's Independence. Delhi is a city raging with religious intolerance – Hindus and Muslims clash. Raj, an ardent Hindu, participates in the riots and slaughter. One night, in a Muslim enclave, he is overpowered. A man, watching from the safety of his home, sees Raj fall in the street, beaten and wounded. The man runs to Raj and drags him inside. The family gives refuge and nurses Raj for days. It is a Christian home. Raj's strong citadel of hate for all non-Hindus crumbles amid the power of love as caring "weakness" energizes his soul. That weakness turns Raj to conversion!

2. Hirendra, a caste Brahmin, honors Hindu obligations. Restlessness stirs in him. His devotion and practice were indeed *"an offering far too small."* He observes the small Christian community in his hometown. Though not prosperous, they are joyful, mutually supportive. Hirendra seeks a place in this new spiritual way when he is transferred to New Delhi; here he finds *"love so amazing, so divine [it] demands his all"* (his old presumptions, his baggage). He experiences grace and peace in covenant fellowship: God-with-him, not God-on-the-fringes.

In Shakespeare's *Julius Caesar*, Brutus commits to assassinate Caesar. This looses in him a spiritual conflict: possibly a right end, surely a wrong means. Brutus returns home from the Senate. He and his wife, Portia, are close, a lifetime of sharing values. Portia senses Brutus' anxiety. Brutus is unable to share the commitment causing his soul's torment; he distances himself from Portia. Portia asks: *"Dwell I but in the suburbs of your leisure?"*

Job's real suffering is not material loss or body sores! Job cannot identify why he feels lost in spiritual darkness. He clings to his self-rightness. He fails to observe he relegates covenant fellowship to some shadowy, future spiritual suburb. His morality is a fortresslike protective wall built on wrongly valued religious rubble.

Job challenges God; God responds. Job abandons his private fortress and centers on living his human experience in a new perspective: fellowship. Job's conclusion becomes a beginning!

A Lenten retreat: look afresh at what kind of "being" I really am? Portia's question is apt: "Does my earth-valued baggage consign God to the suburbs of my spirit?"

97

Meditation Seventeen

Casual observers hardly notice Good Friday/Easter. Life moves on in familiar
rhythms.
Jesus' followers struggle with lingering trauma.
Scripture considers the resurrection central for covenant faith, but it gives few
details of how it happened. The gospels note its impact – rather randomly.
It is not easy to define Jesus' appearance after Easter.
He bids Thomas touch the wounds. Others are told not to touch him.
Jesus is visible as the disciples remember him; he eats fish.
He also seems ethereal – passing through a locked door.
Jesus is accessible for those close to him, but makes no "public" appearance.
He always seems more shadow than substance.
Then comes the Ascension – a great transition, after waiting 40 days.
Disciples are not prepared for a dynamic change:
the risen one is in a form among us, then becomes the Lord abiding in us.
This is a giant step from affirming our beliefs to witnessing our faith!
Now faith is the encounter of God-with-us in some other form.

A Breath of Fresh Air

*When it was evening on the first day of the week, and the doors of the house
where the disciples had met were locked for fear of the Jews, Jesus came and
stood among them and said, "Peace be with you. As the Father has sent me, so
I send you." When he had said this, he breathed on them and said to them,
"Receive the Holy Spirit."* (John 20:19-22)

Crowds fill an auditorium long before the scheduled time. Anticipation of a celebrity's appearance generates excitement. How much longer?

As youngsters in Sunday School we sang: *Hold the Fort for I Am Coming.* We got tired of "holding." Nobody came. Enthusiasm waned. Our cheerleading effort seemed unreal.

We find Jesus' followers on Easter evening. They flee from the empty tomb, out of the garden. They closet in the upper room ... a team huddles, leaderless. Expectations deflate. Wearily, some hike to Emmaus. Some return to Galilee; mending fishing nets to restart the old business.

When spiritual expectations flatten, we slip back into familiar ruts and routines. How quickly temporarily dormant normalcy returns ... even after an Easter event. (Perhaps in a week or two we simply sigh: "Oh well, let's go back to what we know!")

Sadly, easily, we gloss over how shoddy many of our ruts and routines are! It takes committed energy to work through the implications of any new kind of life – especially when we want our life with God to be real. That's the energy in our text. Jesus is present with his disciples. He offers a breath of fresh air as a way out of a me-myself-and-I life – closed, alone.

Jesus calls us to live the bigness life beyond death brings! Does the bigness unnerve us? Is this the part of Easter we run away from? Is this the eerie tomb part?

Where is the <u>new</u> in your life? Is your life a *before* or *after* Easter Gospel?

<u>Before</u>: visions of new and enhanced conditions for life. <u>After</u>: unsure of life changes I might face. Because of Easter, things are now God-sized. God wastes nothing, but how easily we waste God and his grace! We are on the empty-tomb side of Easter, not the Calvary side! This is the ***Alleluia!***

Jesus' initial greeting in the text is: *"Peace be with you."* It's his own peace, not an everyday, worldly version. Jesus continues: *"As the Father sent me, so I send you!"* Then Jesus breathes on those gathered. It's a recurring God-action. God's breath animates matter (dust), Genesis 2:7. Dry bones in Ezekiel 37:9 revive.

In the text, Jesus' breath is a gift-of-himself experience: *"Receive the Holy Spirit."* Jesus doesn't present a written document; he breathes. It's God's covenant exchange for the old life. He claims us as his own, a resurrection fellowship. God inhabits and transforms human aloneness with comfort. It is peace – the comfort of his energy with us. It is empowerment – the claim for fellowship and service.

One wintry Saturday during World War II, I rode with my pastor father while he did church errands and visited members. I sensed he was frustrated: gasoline shortages reduced participation, rationing limited resources. We stopped at Brown's neighborhood grocery store. Dad and Pa Brown sat by the potbellied stove in the back corner. While they chatted I explored – fascinated by the variety and abundance. Dad called; we left. He hummed as we drove. I reflect now: fellowship wakened the claim and comfort that transform anxiety.

Consider a person sitting by the hearth with a friend – just together, never thinking conversation will make life smoother. What happens? One catches the inspiration and energy of another's presence, discovers a look in the other's eyes, then goes out again into a busy world – at peace. So may you and I know God-with-us. It's what you get out of fellowship and what fellowship gets out of you!

Jesus promises: *"I will not leave you orphaned/desolate; I am with you…my peace I give you."* (John 14:27) This peace bears us through troubling devastations. It sustains and fills us with renewing resources.

A few days following Easter, Jesus and his disciples were atop a rise of land. Jesus – in whatever form – passes beyond the disciples' view. Surely that little band felt left desolate!

Might any of them recall other words of comfort Jesus spoke – back *before* the crucifixion? Remember … the promise that the heavenly Father would send the Holy Spirit … in the name of Jesus (i.e., bearing Jesus' Spirit).

It was May 5, 1961; my seminary class was completing its first year of studies. Classes were interrupted, and we gathered around the TV to watch Alan Shepherd rocket 116.5 miles into space at 5,100 mps. He lifted off, and in five minutes his craft splashed down in the Atlantic Ocean. The TV commentator ecstatically cried: *"He came down! He's alive! It's a miracle!"*

Amid the excitement in the room, there was enough silence for all to hear the seminary president's response: *"The miracle is not what went up came down, but what came down went up!"*

Easter needs its natural connection with Ascension Day. God-with-us is now in non-earth form. As the Christmas experience celebrates the Word appearing in human form, so Easter-Ascension witnesses divine presence change from "human" to what we call a "spirit" form. God-with-us moves beyond the conditions of earth, space and time … continuity assured.

I was 13 years old – the summer following my first year in high school. My father arranged a job for me at our denomination's summer camp. It was my first full-time job and a job away from home. I had no idea what it required. What would be expected of me? What skills and competence would I need to fulfill expectations?

Dad drove me to the camp. I moved in, and he turned me over to the manager. Then it was time for him to leave. We walked to the car, bade farewell, slowly the car moved away – Dad was looking back, smiling, waving. I reflect on his departure. He didn't just leave – he made an <u>exchange</u>. In place of his absence, he left his peace … affirmation of my claim as his son! I was empowered; he left himself as part of me. He affirmed he invested everything he was in my life; he entrusted me with that investment – his mark, like a stamp of guarantee in a passbook. In that moment verging on desolation, Dad breathed his life on me, in me. And still I count the dividends of that blessing.

That first Easter night, behind closed doors, Jesus stood looking at the disciples. That visitation continues—he offers a breath of fresh air where we are. He claims, he comforts.

After that evening experience, the disciples' fear didn't matter anymore, or their turning away, or the poor showing they made on Good Friday. By this one undefeated life, the disciples were as great as ever they could bear to be; yes, greater than they might like if they thought about it!

Never again do any of us have to settle for our jumbled store of grim facts. We trust we are God's own, alive in Spirit freshness! That comes with power to redefine the spiritually "real" in all of earth's realities!

That is why for us Easter is now the first day of the week – the beginning time. No one has to settle for the way it's been up to now. Nor do we, not in a reality where Christmas comes out of a stable, the Son of God out of a tradition-oriented village, and 21 centuries of the Body of Christ out of a tomb.

Meditation Eighteen

Pentecost is spiritual action: covenant bonding with God. It confirms our identity *in Christ* until the full revelation of glory.

Jesus' three-year ministry (baptism to ascension) is a dot in the span of history. Pentecost equips the body of Christ to own and bring God's initiatives into our history. Transforming grace continues: an exchange reaching into life beyond death. It has overtones of Christmas anticipation.

The excitement of Christmas: *"We have seen His glory."*

Pentecost's excitement: *"… the glory of this mystery which is Christ in you …"*

The coming of the Holy Spirit is both a *past* event and a *now* event.

Pentecost uniquely celebrates the unity of creation and re-creation.

It seals faith in the living God.

Blessed with Guidance and Courage

Jesus said: "I have said these things to you while I am still with you. But the Advocate, the Holy Spirit, whom the Father will send in my name, will teach you everything, and remind you of all that I said to you....When the Spirit of truth comes, He will guide you into all truth...You will receive power when the Holy Spirit comes to you." (John 14:25-26; 16:13a; Acts 1:8)

On the day of Pentecost, all were filled with the Holy Spirit. (Acts 4:1a,4a)

One body has many members, and these members do not have the same function, so in Christ we who are many form one body. (Romans 12:4b-5a)

Ascension Day marks a vital transition from Christmas to Pentecost. 1) The Son in human form resumes fullness in the God-head. 2) The meaning of *disciple* shifts: from a small inner circle to a wide-ranging fellowship that names Jesus "Lord." This is the Church – Christ's body with a mission to be yeast in all cultures. Paul calls all in this community "children of God."

The term *disciple* implies community members have a twofold identity:

1. Each is God-gifted with unique personal qualities. These are nascent gifts; each must develop and share them cooperatively with others' gifts.

2. Members are a body, a fellowship – a community sharing covenant values and loyalty with one Lord. Individual parts invest in the health and harmony of the whole. Its mission is witness, service, and personal renewal.

This dual identity is stressful. It requires grace to reconcile priorities. Most Christians recall personal dilemmas causing stress. As an adolescent, I identified myself with groups outside my family – friends at school and in social organizations. From time to time a nonfamily group's activity or values conflicted with those of the family. It caused an inner struggle – how to make a choice when any choice might dishonor some loyalty. (I have an individual identity and a shared identity. When they conflict, there is inner stress and social stress.) Scripture recounts such a dilemma:

- Cain's "disconnect" from Abel: *"Am I my brother's keeper?"*
- Naomi and Ruth after Boaz's death:

    Naomi: *"Go back to your people."* (*i.e.*, your native ethnic connection).

    Ruth: *"Don't ask me to leave you."* (*i.e.*, let me keep my new affiliation).

- Jesus sends missioners out in pairs: *"Take nothing with you."* (no support); on their return he asks: *"Did you ever need anything?"* (provision came).

Now we encounter the Pentecost experience: the indwelling Spirit is personal <u>and</u> the Spirit bonds members as a body. Individual identities find unity by sharing gifts/self – a corollary of self-denial Jesus notes (Mark 8:27ff). The Holy Spirit reconciles: the diversity of resources works together for good, i.e., wholeness and healing.

Covenant bonding offers human vessels divine power. The steward is a channel for the master's grace.

Jesus' call to *"deny self"* and *"take up your cross"* now indicates a new outcome: not fear of deprivation but assurance of companionship. The connection weakens the lure of private achievement. *"Take up one's cross"* is a community commitment, not self-concern.

A fanciful story describes a customer shopping. The shopper looks up and discovers God behind the sales counter.

Shopper: *What are you selling?*

God: *What does your heart desire?*

Shopper: *Peace of mind, relief from hurt, security, happiness for one and all.*

God: *I don't sell fruit here, only seeds.*

Pentecost: receiving Spirit breath (John 20:22), godly inspiration that germinates the seed of redemption. The indwelling Spirit-life empowers the church's mission: continuity of God's purposes. One of Paul's grand phrases celebrates this: *"Christ in us, the hope of glory!"* (Col 1:27)

The Holy Spirit enlivens individual gifts and collective gifts. These seed-gifts are sown in stewards, ready for right husbanding. There is the season of ripening – the work of Spirit power. Fruit doesn't appear by magic.

The Holy Spirit is present as our heavenly advocate *(paraklete),* i.e., a guide and counsel for every steward. The *paraklete:*

1) empowers and guides stewards to use resources rightly;

2) encourages and comforts stewards (prods our hesitation).

Pentecost empowers (nurtures) spiritual growth to generate a holy and wholesome quality of life. Jesus notes this with everyday images:

- I am bread: to sustain daily activity of body, mind, spirit.

- I am water: to revive inspiration and initiative in drought times.

- I am life: to model service.

- I am resurrection: to show the promise of belonging, continuity!

Pentecost encourages. We reach out in service that affects material needs and heart hungers. Again, Jesus illustrates this with images of familiar, everyday resources:

- Salt: cleanses, preserves, flavors (zest and radiance).

- Light: make clear what is right and just (not as lamps, but light!).

- Leaven: substantive changes that re-form the way of fulfillment.

Pentecost is a pivotal moment in history. The covenant of Law began in Israel's wilderness. Pentecost seals God's covenant of grace and assures the children of God they would never again be desolate – as often happens when we most acutely feel the crush of daily obligations and anguish.

Josh, 16 years old, and his father often clashed. Confrontations were sparked by generational differences, youthful behavior patterns, and conflicting expectations. One such clash spurred Josh to walk out. The father did nothing for a day or two; then he started to ask around the neighborhood. No results. A week passed, still no contact.

The father recalled Josh used a nearby skateboard facility. The father had a sign painted; in the early afternoon he hung it prominently in the skateboard area. It read:

Josh, I'm sorry. Let's work things out.
If you can forgive me, please meet me here
tomorrow afternoon. Love, Dad

The next day the father went to the park. Josh was sitting there chatting with three others. Josh got up and ran to his father; they embraced.

Father: *Are they friends of yours?*

Josh: *No, but we all have the same name – Josh. I think they read the sign and came expecting - hoping, like me - the message was for them.*

Pentecost is our Father's sign – an ever-fresh message. It's a message for anyone separated or broken. It welcomes the disconnected and separated and heavy-laden in this family, this holy body. The Church presents it everywhere, all the time. The sign first hung at the east gate of Eden long ago. For 2,000 years branches of the family travel the world and replicate the invitation – in Jerusalem, Judea, Samaria, and the nations of the world: *"I am in you as the Holy Spirit, I abide in you in the Holy Spirit – to renew your courage and rightness. Be one with me."*

Meditation Nineteen

All Saints' Day is a 'harvest festival' – it celebrates
the outcomes of redemptive love.
It recognizes good and faithful stewards and their effect in the world.
Some are contemplative: Teresa of Avila, Bernard of Clairvaux.
Some engage in active service: Francis of Assisi, Mother Teresa.
Some are seldom mentioned: parents, missioners.
Saints: those who willingly bear divine holiness.
Holiness is never measured as quantity; it's the natural quality
of life and service for God's stewards.
A saint is a spiritual being whose faith bonds self and Spirit.

Made Whole and
Holy by Love!

How blessed is God! And what a blessing he is!
He's the Father of our Lord, Jesus Christ, and takes us to the high places of
blessing with him. Long before he laid down the earth's foundations, he had us
in mind, had settled on us as the focus of his love, to be made whole and holy
by his love. (Eph 1:3-5, Peterson)

Halloween (All Hallows' Eve) and All Saints' Day have ancient goals: to resolve fears and reaffirm security ... especially amid unseen forces and powers that seem to affect us. Such holidays (holy days) are resting places – a pause to redeem energy – human and spiritual. The energy generates vital inner healing and peace.

As a child, I delighted in a mix of sham-terror and glee when a parent read me scary pieces like James Whitcomb Riley's *Little Orphant Annie* (stanza 2):

> *Wunst they wuz a little boy wouldn't say his prayers –*
> *An' when he went to bed at night, away up-stairs,*
> *His Mammy heerd him holler, an' his Daddy heerd him bawl,*
> *An' when they turn' the kivvers down he wusn't here at all!*
> *An' they seeked him in the rafter-room, an' cubby-hole and press,*
> *An' seeked him up the chimbly flue, an' ever'-wheres, I guess;*
> *But all they ever found wuz thist his pants an' roundabout –*
> *An' the Gobble-ins 'll git you ef you don't watch out!*

We do encounter things that go bump in the night: surprise encounters with spiritlike unknowns, unseen presences in unlit spaces! (Adults also react visibly to the unexpected – all the while pretending bravery.)

One October in the 1960s, Sylvia and I were in the valley of Kashmir. We traveled in a modest-sized propeller aircraft – capable of negotiating the 14,000-foot-high Himalayan pass. A parishioner used Kashmiri hot peppers in her cooking. She requested us to bring some. We boarded our return flight with a 20-pound burlap sack of freshly dried chili peppers. We stowed them in the open, overhead luggage space – by the ventilation blower.

After about 25 minutes into the flight, we sensed something in the air – a very strong, spicy aroma. Before long, it affected everyone in the aircraft: sniffling noses, tearing eyes, sneezing. It was mysterious and discomforting to the senses. The flight crew calmed nerves – visitors to the valley often returned with bundles of chili peppers. (We got off the plane last – making "responsibility" for discomfort as anonymous as possible!)

As adults, we protect our spirit-sensitivities. We seek and test reliable resources. The hero in Thornton Wilder's "The Skin of Our Teeth" ponders what initiatives will restore something good out of war's devastation: *"All I ask is the chance to build new worlds and God has always given us that; and given us voices to guide us; and the memory of our mistakes to warn us."*

So we ask: What voices? What memories? Christians find solace and inspiration from saints – our Pentecost legacy of spiritual heroes. Saints open us to faith-enrichment … mentors of interaction with the holy.

Saints fit two primary categories: 1) Saints whose spiritual gifts merit wide recognition; 2) familiar "heroes," a circle of saintly souls who inspire and affect our personal behavior, actions.

Paul celebrates a vision of the church (Eph 1:3-5). He salutes *"saints in Ephesus."* The word blessing is used. It is: a) God's love acting in human lives; and b) human actions that make faith visible: *"God … settled on us as the focus of his love, to be made whole and holy by his love."*

- God <u>settles</u> on us – as an integral part of our spiritual being!

- God <u>chooses/acts</u> – specific, intentional verbs that give us direction.

Saints accept unearned love – we respond with holy actions that transform.

Reconsider the text. Imagine it's a letter to you from a one-time mentor:

> *I salute you saints – you and your circle of Christian friends. This blessing is not something adrift in the air. I see God is acting among you. God chooses you to be in fellowship – together you generate saving action. It's an old story – for centuries it has come down through your families and heritage. It is stories of God's Spirit touching your lives, enlivening your witness. I see it as a continuing story that makes people whole and holy. It reveals how God's zest restores lives gone bland and fearful.*

The church, the body of Christ: a fellowship of relationships, the whole relying on parts being/doing right.

Our New Delhi church has two cross-topped towers. Taxi drivers all over the city refer to the facility as the "double-crossed" church – "double" increases value, not negates value. A devout Sikh taxi driver we know described "double crossed" this way: *"It is a place of 'double' good: God does good there; people who leave there do good!"*

Each newborn in faith is chosen, made whole and holy. Made whole: refits a person for rightness, realigned! God "rights" us. Made holy: this enables a person to live rightly within this world! The fruit one bears makes this obvious.

All who read this are saints – a fellowship of the whole and holy. Your calling – God's servers – to equip, build up the body.

Saints equip. My seatmate on a flight from New Delhi was retired Field Marshal Carriappa. He inquired about my work; I replied, *"A pastor."* He removed a small card from his wallet. It listed phrases, such as: *"Do unto others as you have them do to you,"* *"Do not boast of yourself, your importance."*

He (a Hindu) presented a card to every soldier he met (as Army Chief-of-Staff). He considered these behaviors essential equipment for soldiers' duty and service. (We concentrate efforts on outreach. One also equips with in-reach!)

Saints build up. The whole and holy ministry touches what is unright! Some happens in the course of daily activity. Some involves conscious intervention. Caring children often show this instinctively. One day a child returned from school later than usual. This brief dialogue ensued:

Mother: *Why are you so late?*
Child: *I had to help someone who was in trouble.*
Mother: *What did you do to help?*
Child: *Oh, I sat down and helped cry.*

We equip and build in the context of earth-life. We transform, with win/win energy. We engage, enhance – salt and spice for the bland, dull.

Sylvia and I arrived at Philadelphia International Airport in the spring of 1972. International drug trade/smuggling was rampant. The customs officer asked why we traveled in Asia. We replied we were missionaries on short home leave. He showed a cross hanging under his shirt: *"I'm a layman here in South Philadelphia. Many of us in our parish feel we have a mission with locals involved in drugs. We, on the other hand, offer young people 'right' to get high on!"* He is a saint offering lives Spirit-flavoring!

Saints are God's stewards. Saints serve, sacrifice, save, salt, spice! They continue the windfall begun the first Pentecost. Saints show self-discipline. Holy action happens when the Lord says: *"Do something"* – and we don't hesitate and offer back talk!

Saints came before us, go with us, come after us. Saints are a cloud of witnesses giving us shade from the world's scorching pressures. Saints are a host of support and direction – mentors looking over the shoulder. If we experience even as few as five such "blessers" in a year, it means some 400 have already been part of this life! And I wonder – right now! – who is looking over a shoulder my way, your way? Be sure to look!

So join the refrain of an All Saints' Day hymn: *"I sing a song of the saints of God ... and I mean to be one too!"*

Meditation Twenty

Faith Abides

…what is perfect will someday appear, and what isn't perfect will then disappear. When we were children, we thought and reasoned as children. But when we grew up, we quit our childish ways. <u>Now</u> all we can see of God is like a cloudy picture in a mirror. <u>Later</u> we will see him face to face. We don't know everything, but then we will, just as God completely understands us. For now there are faith, hope and love. But of these three, the greatest is love. (I Cor 13:10-13, CEV)

Christian faith is a personal response to God's initiatives. The encounter is a covenant exchange. God offers himself for us; we call it grace. We welcome the encounter, and our particular response is to bear God's holiness. Faith ripens a fresh personal identity as a spiritual being. As self opens to God, holiness effects the transition to life *in Christ*.

The encounter continues growth in grace as I benefit from God's investments. Faith makes "spiritual" a more congenial and apt measure *vis-à-vis* what is labeled "real".

It is not a casual gesture to lose an identity (self) and trust that a new identity awaits our acceptance. But that is what the encounter is all about. The hesitancy any may show is not unique to this time and space. It is the very dynamic of God-with-us initiatives: 1) Jesus' life and ministry, crucifixion; 2) the resurrected Christ's ascension; and 3) the Lord's return as the indwelling Holy Spirit. This deepens our understanding of God's nature and its rightness for us. Responding to the initiatives changes lives and ways of living.

Paul affirms that faith "abides." It seems a carefully chosen word; it aptly confirms his own experience. Paul's Greek term expressed in the English word "abide" indicates the constant state of something in and through time, in and through space. It affirms something is whole, continues without change, with constancy, becomes perfect.

Paul speaks of how God-with-us affects a person of faith. We experience a transition from identifying our nature as self to life *in Christ*. Then comes Paul's spirit-charged passage on love (I Cor 13). The chapters following are Paul's bold witness of a grand (and perfecting) transition: life, death, and life beyond death. This connects every element of God's investment in us – our human encounter with him as Lord and Spirit. What abides of the encounter is our own initiatives – what we do with grace and gifts. From the divine-human exchange comes our stewardship of faith, love, hope.

In the passage from I Corinthians on the previous page, two words are underlined: <u>Now</u> and <u>Later</u>.

Paul indicates a clear distinction: now = at the moment; later = on the other hand, at that fullness of time.

Now begins at Pentecost – the experience of God-with-us as Holy Spirit. This Spirit works initiatives of healing, wholeness, reconciliation, re-creation.

This recurs over and over in human time and space – extending rapidly beyond the local sites of Judea and Galilee.

Spiritual beings witness their new identity for any and all who feel God-forsaken.

We celebrate bearers of holiness. God sanctifies every life *in Christ*, the assurance of *Christ in me*.

This experience shapes who we are, how we live, and how we perceive death. It's an experience we affirm in this chorus:

> *Spirit of the living God, fall afresh on me.*
> *Spirit of the living God, fall afresh on me.*
> *Melt me, mold me, fill me, use me.*
> *Spirit of the living God, fall afresh on me.*

It's a promise God fulfills; it's an initiative happening. Our life *in Christ* assures continuity – a transition beyond the limits of our time and space.

Response to the continuum of divine initiatives and divine presence is called faith. By faith, I live earth time/space *in Christ*. I experience God as creator, re-creator, and sustainer. This is the "born again" experience Jesus described to Nicodemus (John 3). The new life is life by God's re-creation. Paul explains it another way in Galatians 2:20 ff (Peterson):

> *Christ lives in me. The life you see me living is not "mine,"*
> *but it is lived by faith in the Son of God, who loved me and*
> *gave himself for me. I am not going to go back on that.*

This is covenant life, a holy exchange: God bonding with each "new born" image-of-God. Grace works re-creation in and through us. This replaces a self-soul I let go – the self I deny, the soul I lose (cf Mark 8:27ff). The new self is a spiritual being energized by the Holy Spirit. The soul that comes with the new birth is one where idea and feeling and action (mind, heart, and might) are reconciled to work together for good. They are no longer rivaling personal characteristics. They are mutually dependent traits, not elements contending for priority. The catalyst is God's energy that we call "love," Believers claim a new belonging – the action noted in John 1:12-13 (note the key verb, <u>receive</u>):

> *...to all who <u>received</u> him, who believed in his name, he gave*
> *power to become children of God, who were born, not of blood*
> *or the will of the flesh or of the will of man, but of God.*

At the end of John's Gospel (John 20:22) the Lord says: _Receive the Holy Spirit_. "Receive" here is an imperative action: "take to oneself, take in hand, claim." This is our part in the covenant exchange – lay claim and make God's initiatives one's own. This is like receiving a guest in your home – extending benefits of its resources. (Recall the powerful image of the Lord standing outside the door waiting to be let in. Rev 3:20)

Grace works re-creation in and through us. Paul affirms this covenant exchange experience in I Cor 2:12: "... _we have received not the spirit of the world, but the Spirit that is from God, so that we may understand the gifts bestowed on us by God._" We know and show the God-provided benefits (cf Psalm 103:1-2).

Many have special spiritual experiences. Perhaps a "heat-of-the-moment" revival event that cools amid the pressures and urgency of career and family. Now, in this senior-time, we may sense not-quite-complete spiritual peace. It is a good 'itch' to heed. Choose to be ready for what's ahead – that's strength, not weakness. Mature spiritual exploration appeals. Revisit the Word of God for encounter, not just quick relief for spiritual discomforts.

The Word of God inspires. Inspiration is a "happening" in which God's initiatives enrich the spiritual being. It is the experience of God's presence, a recurring revival in the church's history. Inspired persons intuitively know God's presence. Life experience takes on fresh color and vibrancy. Inspiration moves faith from beliefs to fellowship.

Inspiration – God's breath, God's life-giving spirit – isn't fanciful whimsy. It is God's energy. It generates results. We sing of the experience.

Breathe on me, breath of God, fill me with life anew,
that I may love what thou does love, and do what thou wouldst do.

The exploration is an enterprise – a purposeful engagement of vision and commitment. Faith **works** in me. What does it do? Faith enlivens my spirit to more excellent human interaction. As I walk the disciple walk, ongoing Scripture reading highlights what is right. Jesus' assessments of people and situations exude rightness. Jesus' call for change is healing therapy. I realize old ways and behaviors _seem_ right – but hang onto earthly patterns. I am ready to take on more holy initiatives.

Faith calls me to a particular stewardship: the practice of love. Is there a catalog of loving practices? Perhaps somewhere. There is no catalog of fixed applications. We learn to recognize fresh opportunities and invest in them. Faith reveals what I overlooked previously.

Affairs are more clearly soul-size! This carries forward our exploration into God. It brings us to explore self as bearing God's nature. It is surely an expanded experience of inspiration.

Meditation Twenty-One stimulates readiness for inspiration, the grace that opens us to God's energy. Its harvest is stamina for the soul.

Meditation Twenty-One

Genesis begins with a void, an abyss – formless, lightless.
Then an overreaching sensation: "brooding."
It is God's presence – power (an entity, not just a product).
God speaks, energy works – a Word utters "Light!"
Light happens. Invisible sound begets visible light.
Jesus' imperative *"You must be born again"* unnerved Nicodemus.
Biological birth is not repeatable.
God broods, or, Spirit hovers.
Energy replicates the Word: power creates, or transforms.
The creator/re-creator broods: "Be", and "Be born again."
Love's Word brings dust alive as a human – able to respond,
receive and steward this love.

The Brooding Spirit

First this: God created the Heavens and Earth – all you can see, all you don't see. Earth was a soup of nothingness, a bottomless emptiness, an inky blackness. God's spirit brooded like a bird above the watery abyss. God spoke: "Light!" And light appeared. God saw that light was good and separated light from dark.

(Genesis 1:1-3, Peterson)

The Word was first, the Word present to God, God present to the Word. He was in the world, the world was there through him, and yet the world didn't even want him. But whoever did want him, who believed he was who he claimed and would do what he said, He made to be their true selves, their child-of-God selves. These are the God-begotten, not blood-begotten, not flesh-begotten, not sex-begotten. The Word became flesh and blood, and moved into the neighborhood. We saw the glory with our own eyes, the one-of-a-kind glory, like Father, like Son. Generous inside and out, true from start to finish. (John 1:1,10-14, Peterson)

<u>Who</u> is at the beginning. *"In the beginning, God."* (Gen 1:1) Then <u>what.</u> In Hebrew – *tohu-wa-bohu*, nothingness, emptiness, blackness, unmeasured, unformed cosmos (Gen 1:2). This is desolation, but not just itself! Above and around and through the *tohu-wa-bohu* is nonvisible awareness, God's energy, life-breath. The Hebrew image: "spirit brooding" – caring anticipation of something wanted, like an eagle nesting eggs – anticipating community and continuity.

God speaks (Gen 1:3); action has definition. God speaks: *"Light!" And light appeared!* The Word has intention: transform *tohu-wa-bohu*. In time, God shapes a creature and gives it His breath – it lives. God embeds in the creature something unique – capacity to interact with creator God. In all creation, only the human is competent to share in this spirit-encounter.

Genesis 1:1-3 introduces: 1) the creative Source; 2) the life-generating Word; and 3) sustaining Spirit-power. God's energy fulfills its intention with three modes. And so the saga commences.

The Old Testament describes Israel's meandering, out of slavery. The "nation" lacks cultural identity – and models. It becomes self-absorbed. It tries to identify the Word's intention with words in the Law. That reduces interactions to legal obligations. It misses God's dynamic encounter. Spirit and Word still brood, waiting for the right time; prophetic visions keep anticipation alive.

A prophet laments: *"I [God] distance myself from your feasts and solemn assemblies. Away with your praise music! Let justice roll on like a river and righteousness like a never-ending stream!"* (Amos 5:21,23a,24, Peterson). This cry doesn't resonate with the people who live a Spirit-less, level-earth, human-absorbed existence. The Creator intends Israel to beam His extravagant power in the world; "His" people opt for low-wattage energy to conserve self-purity.

Fast-forward to John's Gospel. Its opening echoes Gen 1:3 (Peterson):

The Word was God, in readiness from day one. He was in the world, the world was there through him and yet the world didn't even notice. He came to his own people, but they didn't want him. But whoever did want him, who believed he was who he claimed, he made to be their true selves, their child-of-God selves.

A new beginning: The Word comes in the form of a person and re-creates. Energy now touches humans' inner *tohu-wa-bohu* and reforms new souls from that dust and ashes.

Let us follow some Word-human encounters noted in John's Gospel.

1) Jesus meets John the Baptist at the Jordan River (John 1). The Baptist tells his followers: "*[Jesus is] the one – God's brooding Spirit is on him and he brings redemptive power to any who will receive.*" The Spirit stirs. Commonplace encounters the holy.

2) Jesus at Cana in Galilee – a wedding (John 2). Water reserved for ritual necessity becomes wine for joyful spontaneity. John indicates that a sign reveals the character of the one doing it. The holy affects the commonplace.

3) Passover, Jesus visits the Temple in Jerusalem (John 2:13ff). Here, Israel (through its priests, behind the veil) "encounters" God. The temple's flourishing sacrifice business relies on a daily supply of fresh doves. Jesus cleanses the temple. Jesus' defense: "*Destroy the temple* [the point of God-man communion] *– it will be put together again in three days.*" Jewish authorities sneer at Jesus' defense: a claim of inner grace. Many do accept Jesus' spiritual authority.

4) Nicodemus, a bemused senior Pharisee, finds Jesus' signs unsettling (John 3). He comes at night (the image of his own numbing, inner darkness). Jesus' talk is personal – not generic, liturgical words. Nicodemus seems caught in a rut, his old ideas niggle: "*My old-time religious belief lacks something. Is it a future? Inside I'm all tohu-wa-bohu. Traditional temple-talk isn't effective; my beliefs are no sail to catch the 'wind' (Spirit!) moving me Godward!*"

Jesus tells Nicodemus he must "*begin again*" to perceive how God blesses and redeems. So Nicodemus asks: "*How can anyone be born who has already been born and grown up?*" Jesus answers: "*Unless a person submits to Spirit-brooding [let the invisible revive the visible] it's not possible to enter God's kingdom [to know God as Lord].*"

How does one handle this? Would the brooding spirit ever move Nicodemus out of his doldrums?

And what about any spiritual routines? Are they ruts of pious repetition that miss renewing, brooding Spirit-power?

5) Jesus is in Galilee – Sychar, Jacob's Well (John 4). He is tired, thirsty. A Samaritan woman comes. (Samaritans are "separated brethren.") John condenses the conversation:

Jesus: *Would you give me a drink of water?*
Woman: *How come you, a Jew, ask me, a Samaritan woman, for a drink?*
Jesus: *If you know God's generosity and who I am, you would ask **me** for a drink. ... I'd give you fresh, living water.*
Woman: (Does this Jew consider himself greater than Jacob?) *You don't even have a bucket.* (More verbal shadow-boxing, but something brooding nudges in.)
Jesus: *Call your husband.* (This flashing thrust of a personal matter touches her to the quick. She shifts to a more neutral topic.)
Woman: *We Samaritans worship here at Mount Gerizim; you Jews say worship is at Jerusalem.*
Jesus: (Jesus makes religious form personal!) *The time is coming when what matters before God is who you are, the way you live. ... God is Spirit. ... Those who worship him must do so out of their spirit.*
Woman: *Well, I don't know about that. But I know the Messiah is coming. When he comes, we'll get the whole story.*
Jesus: (The encounter!) *I am he. You don't have to wait any longer.*
(She goes and tells villagers who return, hear Jesus, and believe. The brooding Spirit's gift: reorientation of time and space – from past to future, from history to inheritance, new life for old.)

6) Jesus is back in Cana (John 4:46ff). A Roman official knows Jesus' signs and seeks Jesus. The Roman soldier perceives this power as mercy, a redeemer who serves. (Worshippers in Roman religious practice serve self-absorbed gods.) The officer's child is at home, dying. Agitated by his own inner *tohu-wa-bohu*, the Roman pleads: *"Come! It's life or death!"* Jesus says: *"Go, your son lives."*

These encounters would be judgmental, except each links with a redeeming alternative. Whenever Christ questions our contentment with the spiritually shoddy, he offers cleansing grace. It's a rescue from any form of piety that domesticates people to its terms. A fresh Spirit-wind re-creates, leaving its identifying seal as a new heart/soul, marked with a cross. It bonds faith's response to God's initiatives. And this is as close as God comes to writing his name.

These personal encounters in John resonate with our own stories:
- Nicodemus: rightness dried-up, lacking re-creating energy.
- A Samaritan woman: futility of allegiance to self-limiting expectations.
- A Roman official: horizontal authority open to vertical energy.

It's a rescue from afar off when resources seem to run out, when life's unfullness overwhelms.

John concludes his Gospel's prologue (1:14) affirming this:

Whoever did want him, who believed he was who he claimed
and would do what he said, he made to be their true selves,
their child-of-God selves. The Word became flesh and blood,
and moved into the neighborhood. We saw the glory with our
own eyes, generous inside and out, true from start to finish.

The brooding Spirit creates/births, re-creates/rebirths. Always seeking: bounding over walls, penetrating barriers, impervious to our self-protecting filters. Love's Word touches formlessness in all its guises. We use so much effort to find God. Perhaps we yearn to encounter the Word that moves into any neighborhood overwhelmed by *tohu-wa-bohu.* Its brooding presence can warm every anxious, waiting image-of-God – you, me.

So begins the Church's story: encounters with the re-creating Word (a voice from a hill far away) moving where it will. In three days, God's brooding Spirit-power put brokenness together, and the glory reaches globally.

Seniors especially should welcome an ever-fresh experience of the brooding-Spirit. It's love happening in and for us. Love sets life in motion toward a future that is always beginning. It fills the world with angel presence healing the anguish of human hurts.

Exploration II

Love

The Incarnation is God's wondrous redeeming initiative: God-with-us in Jesus and the Holy Spirit. Faith is our response. It marks our ownership of Paul's new life *in Christ* and Teilhard's new identity as spiritual beings. The transition changes our role in the human experience.

Jesus' ministry connects physical (biological) and spiritual (biographical) change. Jesus points beyond physical forms to less visible initiatives of love:

1) Recall the words of the woman in a crowd (Luke 11:27-28):

> Woman: *Blessed is the woman that bore you and the breasts that nursed you!*

> Jesus: *Blessed rather are those who hear the word of God and obey it.*

2) When doubting Thomas must see/touch scars of the Crucifixion, Jesus offers another valid experience: *"Blessed are those who have not seen and yet have come to believe."* (John 20:29)

3) Jesus calls Nicodemus to a spiritual rebirth – not biological (John 3).

The modern mindset seems to prefer more scientifically based commitments.

Our identity as a spiritual being calls for a new bravery. Or is it actually an "old" bravery – like one Jesus summoned? Consider Mark 10:13-15 (Peterson):

> *The people brought children to Jesus, hoping he might touch them. The disciples shooed them off. But Jesus was irate and let them know it: "Don't push these children away. Don't ever get between them and me. These children are the very center of life in the kingdom. Mark this: Unless you accept God's kingdom in the simplicity of a child, you'll never get in."*

Childlike openness brings one into God's domain, kingdom. (The particular meaning of *domain/kingdom* is "a sphere of influence." Jesus implies a grander dimension: encounter with God opens entry to the kingdom.) Jesus indicates trust/faith brings spiritual beings a new order for action.

Faith connects us to a wellspring of love. New awareness (of God, others, and self) reveals the immense diversity of love. This wakens new behavior, new service ... actions that transform and redeem. Our affairs are now soul-size. *"The simplicity of a child"* means those of us who are no longer children reset a basis and readiness to love and be loved. We pause before we raise reasons to defer caring.

God's initiatives (actions called "love") beget our visible initiatives of love. Our call to **be** and **do** right establishes God's standard more pointedly than laws.

There is no catalog of loving actions, *e.g.*, donate to the food bank. So we explore qualities (innate or adopted) that give love the right form.

Life *in Christ* brings new behaviors: *We love because God first loved us.* (I John 4:19) We discern holy goals, healing interactions – each an example of the overarching verb "to love." Note passages where Jesus shows how love extends personal rightness beyond the measure of law: Matt 5:21ff, Matt 5:40ff, Matt 5:43ff. Love gives actions color, value.

Jesus never ends an interaction saying, *"Go and live happily ever after!"* The Lord never endorses a "just-as-I-am" self-as-self. Jesus' "good news" expects change (which itself is action!). Consider Jesus' dialogue with a religious scholar in Luke 10:25ff (Peterson's version):

Scholar: *Which is the most important of all the commandments?*

Jesus: *The first in importance is 'Listen, Israel: The Lord your God is one; so love the Lord God with all your passion and prayer and intelligence and energy.' [Deut 6:5] And here is the second: 'Love others as well as you love yourself.' [Lev 19:18] There is no other commandment that ranks with these.*

Scholar: *A wonderful answer, Teacher! Why, that's better than all offerings and sacrifices put together.*

Jesus: *You're almost there, right on the border of God's kingdom.*

The law of love becomes the work (energy) of love. Jesus makes love a life-event, a happening. Law takes a person near the *"border"*; love carries the believer across the border, into "God's kingdom" – where the fruits of faith abound. Jesus continues with the parable of a Good Samaritan.

Innocence is a childlike quality, a capacity for uncomplicated human connections. Without notice we lose that. We noted earlier, it begins subtly, that first time anyone asks: *"Am I loved?"* Is that when we turn inside ourselves?

Our 21st-century culture is uneasy with this innocence, preferring fact-based cautions more than faith-based initiatives. Such hesitancy diminishes the soul; one's identity shapes *"outside Christ."*

This separation of sacred and secular keeps self near the *"border of God's kingdom"* – and affairs are not yet soul-size. Faith empowers the self to share the fruits of grace. We can hear Paul say: *"The only thing that counts is faith made effective through love."* (Gal 4:6b)

Jesus endorses the primacy of Deuteronomy 6:5; love now becomes action. Energy merges from the soul's three faculties: mind (forms ideas), heart (clarifies feeling), strength/might (prompts and channels relevant action). Faith sparks this energy.

The soul is the place where the sparking initiative happens. The ideas in Deuteronomy are valid for our modern contexts. The mind produces ideas. The heart tempers feelings to be appropriate. Might/strength is the physical ability and spiritual will to apply initiatives appropriately.

The psalmist prays a real human need: *Create in me a clean heart, O God, and put a new and right spirit within me.* (Ps 51:10) Subsequently, Jeremiah notes God's response: God promises to write His law in people's hearts, and remember their sin no more. (Jer 31:33-34) A few decades later God specifies the intention: *"I will put my spirit within you."* (Ezekiel 36:26-27). There is a new mechanism for expressing faith: hearts of flesh replacing hearts of stone. It's all about a change of heart/soul/spirit – the inner God-welcoming part of us. Let's note something of these three elements of soul.

Mind. A capacity to identify and define observed needs. A defined need leads to a constructive/creative solution – <u>what</u> action is apt, right.

Heart. A mechanism to assess feelings and shape attitudes. This assures an action is appropriate for the need we deal with (neighbor). Is it morally right: in terms of the a) relationships involved; b) the effect it can/will have? This shows <u>why</u> the action is valid, appropriate.

Strength. The intent of love is redemptive action – energy (physical, spiritual, emotional, intellectual). Strength is the way an intention fulfills a need. It is not preset impulses. Strength is <u>how</u> our intention benefits another.

<u>What</u> and <u>why</u> and <u>how</u> depend on perceiving clearly who receives this love – the audience. Is it appropriate for the person, and is it appropriate in the situation/context?

What is the action (love)? We identify a receiver's need.

Why is it right and important? We consider as accurately as possible the effect, benefit.

How does this happen? We use resources for right action/effect.

At this point we observe Jesus' guiding measure: "*...as well as you love yourself.*" Most of us are quite skilled at satisfying our own needs – aptly, promptly, agreeably. Might the skills we use to assess self-satisfaction and rightness influence acts of love for others?

"Neighbor" is a very general designation. It can be someone close, very familiar, and Jesus deals with that often. In the Good Samaritan parable, Jesus broadens the scope. It is not an existing connection. It is alertness both of observation and sensitivity to activity about us in order to see opportunities for love. We observe: need, urgency, resources, personal competence, dignity of the injured. Response requires more than information; it tests the observer's character.

Love is stewardship. Childlike simplicity is never contrived. By faith the steward knows the Master's passion, purpose, and resources to assure acts of love are fruitful.

The steward's <u>work</u> is God's work; it may seem a childlike insight, but it is never childish. The good and faithful steward finds the right <u>jobs</u> to achieve God's calling. It keeps us alert to who we encounter as "neighbor" – the person, the audience, the receiver of loving action.

The steward's job is to make God's love visible – actions that ransom, heal, restore, forgive. The steward works jobs <u>out of self</u>, rather than work self <u>out of a job</u>.

Our work: equip others to prosper God's work. Recall Paul's power-filled plea (Phil 4:1, 7, 11-13):

> *I ... beg you to lead a life worthy of the calling to which you have been called. ... Each of us was given grace according to the measure of Christ's gift ... to equip the saints for the work of ministry, for building up the body of Christ – until all of us come to the unity of faith ... to maturity, to the measure of the full stature of Christ.*

Paul identifies the <u>work</u>: *the unity of faith [covenant bonding]*. Paul categorizes the <u>jobs</u> – *equip the saints* and *build up the body*. Tasks come and go. Jobs (rightly formed) have more continuity. Paul presents a radical challenge (I Cor 14:1, Peterson): *Give yourselves to the gifts God gives you.* Don't claim gifts as our own – a spiritual being knows gifts are used to redeem. Love transforms gifts' features into benefits.

In Gal 5:22, Paul speaks of the fruits of the Spirit, i.e., natural outcomes of stewardship (life *in Christ*). This catalog of fruits of the Spirit is familiar: love, joy, peace, patience, kindness, generosity, faithfulness, gentleness, and self-control. These show what/why/how gifts are loving. The fruits give form, texture, quality, appeal, and vitality to all acts of love. To reshape gifts as love makes life different … not necessarily easier!

Paul continues in Gal 5:25f (Peterson):

> *Since … we have chosen the life of the Spirit, let us make sure that we do not just hold it as an idea in our heads or a sentiment in our hearts, but work out the implications in every detail of our lives. That means we do not compare ourselves with each other as if one of us were better and another worse. … Each of us is an original.*

Faith becomes self-absorbing unless it initiates acts of love. Change faith energy into "happenings!" Faith becoming love generates endless beauty – appeal. Love is faith's savor, unique sensation – obvious both in its presence **and** absence! (Jesus devalues salt lacking savor, it is trod underfoot like gravel.)

Love is a complicated word and action. We can identify some basic characteristics. Most love involves a dynamic, mutual (or shared) relationship. There is emotional and spiritual bonding. (In marriage partnerships, it extends to include physical intimacy.) These kinds of love require reciprocity, shared intentions. It applies to close friendship (of either/both sexes), work associates, those bonded in common activities and causes.

The more idealistic selfless love is an initiative that doesn't imply or require a comparable response … and it need not be anonymous or secretive. Its mark is its particular intention, e.g., the Good Samaritan's action brings relief and succor. The service is selfless; it anticipates no personal return or ongoing bonding. Selfless love is seldom totally "selfless": the self is involved, but not for ego needs.

This perspective is important for the great commandment's tripart connection: love God, love neighbor, love self. Each is part of love as a holy quality. We are not alone! We discover how our spiritual exploration bonds us more closely with God (John 14:18ff):

> *I will not leave you orphaned [alternate translation: desolate]. I'm coming back. In just a little while the world will no longer*

see me, but you're going to see me because I am alive and you're about to come alive. At that moment you will know that I'm in the Father, and you're in me, and I'm in you.

Live a day at a time. Attend to what you can handle with ease, grace and rightness. Strengthen ties in the grand arena of interdependence. God gives us a new spirit/soul; it abounds with noble qualities. Season your faith afresh day-by-day. Paul shares a "spice rack" of qualities that keep initiatives of love from losing their savor (Phil 4:8-9, Peterson):

> *Summing it all up, friends, I'd say you'll do best by filling your minds and meditating on things true, noble, reputable, authentic, compelling, gracious – the best, not the worst; the beautiful, not the ugly; things to praise, not things to curse. Put into practice what you learned from me, what you heard and saw and realized. Do that and God, who makes everything work together, will work you into his most excellent harmonies.*

We come again to our life *in Christ* and *Christ in me*. Let this pulse of life claim you; then, you claim its energy – love. Paul reckons now is the right time – a fullness of time, an apt time (Gal 4:4).

The following ***Meditations*** consider how faith equips us with measures and qualities to assure loving initiatives are right. Micah 6:8 names some such qualities of love (Peterson's version):

> *But [God] already made it plain how to live, what to do,*
> *what God is looking for in men and women.*
> *It's quite simple: Do what is fair and just to your neighbor,*
> *be compassionate and loyal in your love,*
> *And don't' take yourself too seriously –*
> *take God seriously.*

We consider in greater depth the impact of covenant transformed from "old" to "new," especially its clear directive to love. The old covenant "love as law" is born again to be "love as grace." Love of God resonates with love of neighbor, and these both resonate with a followership that honors self *in Christ*.

131

Jesus' healing ministry is an array of wondrous, loving actions.
Each relieves some burdensome dependency:
like a cripple waiting to be carried to the moving waters.
Healing—physical, spiritual—wakens consciousness of power beyond self –
faith, new or renewed.
Faith energizes believers to initiate acts of love.
Loving actions bring benefits of what is holy and healthy.
Seniors' maturity stirs a desire to share spiritual riches.
Opportunities to be loving may seem unimportant,
but every loving act relieves some heart-hunger.
Turn your faith into acts of love; a person all wrapped up in self is
the smallest package in the world.

Hearts Bearing Holiness
Keep the Body Healthy

Jesus said, "Be perfect ... as your heavenly Father is perfect." (Matthew 5:48)
Paul writes: "... it is Christ who lives in me." (Galatians 2:20b)
Jesus said to a crowd, "If any want to become my followers, let them deny themselves and take up their cross and follow me." (Mark 8:34)
Therefore, since we are surrounded by so great a cloud of witnesses, let us lay aside every weight and the sin that clings closely, and let us run with perseverance the race that is set before us. (Hebrews 12:1)

Dylan Thomas shares a charming boyhood memory in *A Child's Christmas in Wales:* "One Christmas was so much like another that I can never remember whether it snowed for 6 days and 6 nights when I was 12 or whether it snowed for 12 days and 12 nights when I was 6."

Everyone treasures precious life experiences – even though we struggle to recall details correctly! Memories are important and cherished. They connect life-values in our human journey. We find/establish values when critical events or moments embed something important in the soul. Values enrich us and improve our skill to use personal gifts and qualities. Every good and faithful steward knows miracle moments. (They are "miracle" because we acknowledge them as out-of-the-ordinary, God-with-us actions.)

As preteens, we try to be Jesus' little sunbeams. We categorize behaviors: <u>Do</u> and <u>Don't</u>! Normal development introduces skills for self-control. Praise encourages us to do right things <u>and</u> do things rightly! We grow – hopefully – in stature, wisdom, and favor (with God, with people)! Gradually, each establishes a "self" accountable for choices.

At some point (perhaps during an early adolescent identity struggle), I encountered Jesus' teaching *"Be perfect!"* (Matt 5:8). This ideal wiggled its way into choices I faced – one after another! In teen years, the ethic was often challenged by a bombardment of less-than-preferred choices. The ethic confused what brought visible or invisible acceptance. A peer focus: Be <u>good</u> in socially connected activities – teams, talents, achievement. A different <u>good</u> in more private achievement, recognition. Teen morality preferred ethical flexibility.

Eventually, I perceived *"Be perfect"* is a value beyond simplistic right or wrong. It extends beyond here-and-now choices. It defines how I begin actions as well as their outcomes. It indicates a correct readiness to act. Am I prepared to have grace be part of my actions? Grace: always whole, complete, ripe. *"Be perfect ... as our heavenly Father is perfect!"* Grace is this kind of rightness waiting to work in us. When I accept grace, I am more than self-as-self. Self now bears God's wholeness and holiness!

Christians try to deal with grace as if it comes in a human variety – using a personal measure of quantity and quality. As sinners (albeit forgiven), do we put a dosage limit on grace? (Might a "co-pay" element be attached – a tension and lingering remnant of old covenant legalism?)

New covenant faith affirms: *"I no longer live, but Christ in me"* (Gal 2:20). Grace is not innate in the "self"; it is God's initiative striving to bear fruit in us! Grace is amazing when we know it as personal experience – peace within, assurance in fellowship. Communion generates love! We sing it:

> *There is a place of full release, near to the heart of God;*
> *a place where all is joy and peace, near to the heart of God.*

This communion frees us to let grace grow us to *"be perfect"*. 1) We accept the breath of God's spirit-wind (an action echoing Jeremiah's anticipation that God would *"etch"* his will on the heart). 2) We live as Christ's new creation – image-bearers.

All parts of us mature (ripen): body, mind, spirit. The fickle, restless, love-seeking heart of the old self (ego), transforms to be love-giving (God-in-us). And nothing separates us from that love. It is not a loan but a trust for stewards. This frees us from fear – even death. Faith repositions death as transition, not finality! Discipleship (*learning* His way) becomes followership (*stewarding* His way). Jesus invites us to trust and obey (accept) this new inner bonding. He presents it to his inner circle at the transfiguration (Mark 8:34):

- *Deny [the old] self* – act in response to the new-heart within.
- *Take up the cross* – accept new conventions for your allegiance.
- *Follow me* – be God's living body!

Our Lord's Supper Collect prayer embraces this expectation: *"Almighty God, unto whom all hearts are open ... cleanse our hearts by the indwelling of your Holy Spirit, that we may <u>perfectly</u> love thee ..."* Such perfect love is a happening, it is our actions, stewardship fully expressed.

Paul gives energy to this with his image of Christians as Christ's living body. We rebirth as the body of Christ moving, comforting and healing, lifting and sharing wherever "local" is.

Each part pools its identity and energy in the body. Our mission and ministry: bring creation the healing and reconciliation for which it groans. An individual's service strengthens the body's witnessing power. (This kind of <u>addition</u> is a quite different from accumulating names on the membership roll!) This is not easy in our time and culture. Few of us feel competent and confident to lose "self" willingly in a raggedy Christ Corps!

There is a glorious image in Hebrews 12:1: ... *we are surrounded by such a cloud of witnesses.* Greek writers used the word "cloud" in two ways: 1) literally (visible, air-borne moisture); and 2) metaphorically (a visible gathering of similar persons/things). The metaphor is drawn from Greek amphitheaters filled for political, athletic, and cultural events with thousands of white-robed citizens.

Eugene Petersen's translation (Heb 12:1) in *The Message* captures the impact of this gathered body. *Do you see what this means – all these pioneers who blazed the way, all these veterans cheering us on …*

Urged by the "cloud" of forebears, we minister and extend the redemptive blessing of love. Our service continues: to find and rebuild waste places (lives, relationships, separations), to redeem those nudged to life's fringes!

I sense this empowerment and encouragement in my pastoral ministry. I am surrounded by a "presence" when I prepare and offer any preaching endeavor. I am enhanced by a cloud of image-bearers, pulpit veterans – they shape and nurture me:
  - Charles Smyth, my preacher father.
  - Charles Sayre, a mentor in my early ministry.
  - Vernon Kooy, my New Testament professor and spiritual mentor.
  - Howard Hageman, my homiletics mentor in seminary.
  - Paul Shearer, George Buttrick, whose master classes refined skills, style.

Their insights orient my <u>followership</u>: how I connect the shepherd's message with the flock – gathered, lost, or wandering.

From this heritage rises our celebration of perfected love. This witness works to redeem those fearing life and death. This love is an alternative to loneness – an addictive first step to be self-absorbed, imprisoned by circumstances (hurting and unique as they are). We gather those who feel alone – to discover they are not alone! How blithely William Wordsworth expresses this:

> *I wandered lonely as a cloud*
> *That floats on high o'er vales and hills,*
> *When all at once I saw a crowd,*
> *A host, of golden daffodils,*
> *Beside the lake, beneath the trees,*
> *Fluttering and dancing in the breeze.*

For often when on my couch I lie
In vacant or in pensive mood,
They flash upon that inward eye
Which is the bliss of solitude;
And then my heart with pleasure fills,
And dances with the daffodils.

Christians bond in <u>followership</u> – an earth-circling "cloud" of image-bearers. It forms and moves by the Holy Spirit; it celebrates some 2,000 years in a journey for eternity. We minister and live (like dancing daffodils!) amid 7 billion of God's people-varieties. We keep fresh the tradition of forebears' comfort and encouragement.

People around the globe thank the Christian community for feeding the poor, housing the homeless, clothing the naked, doctoring/nursing the unwell, finding lost identities hiding under bridges and in drains. That is all generic. The specific – in every instance – is a person loving another person in the name of Jesus Christ. Our love-in-action celebrates God's promise of glory yet to be revealed. I don't know if any loving act of mine has ever altered a statistic. But then, love cannot be calculated that way!

Richard of Chichester (1197-1253) offered this prayer as a member in our Lord's body (a "cloud"):

Thanks be to thee, O Lord, Christ, for all the benefits which
thou has given us; for all the pains and insults which thou hast
borne for us.
O most merciful redeemer, friend and brother, may we know
thee more clearly, love thee more dearly, and follow thee more
nearly; for thine own sake.

Society frames laws that apply equally to all in its jurisdiction.
Morality evolves from sacred and secular experiences rooted in the history of
those belonging to that cultural tradition.
Modern preferences distinguish between secular and religious matters.
Mature faith resists a stark separation of justice and rightness –
whether the reason for "separation" is academic, legal or practical.
A senior's quest: faith that allows love to determine meaning and form.
Love offered is a quality of witness (evangelism).
Wholeness is rarely a casual blending of something just and something right;
they require a proportioned match of need and intention.
What is just and right becomes energy to nurture healing.
Law may be just, but impervious to grace … and miss its own goals.

Justice and Rightness – a Sacramental Union

Let justice fall down like waters and righteousness like an ever-flowing stream.
(Amos 5:24)

It was the late 1940s. I was in high school. My father invited a pastor friend, Rev. Dick Francis, to preach at the church Dad was serving. Our guest always wore a clerical collar (unusual for Methodist pastors at that time). His parish was in the heart of Brooklyn, New York. He learned clerical dress was an asset, an instant identity in Brooklyn's multicultural, multireligious, multiethnic, secular/sacred mix. As we ate Sunday dinner, he told an amusing incident related to his "collar."

Driving down a familiar street in Brooklyn, his mind wandered. He drove through a stop sign; a whistle blared shrilly. A police patrolman approached from behind the car. At the driver's window, he spotted Dick's clerical collar and said (with a thick Irish brogue): *"Father, you went through a stop sign. I won't ticket you, but be careful – the patrolman at the next corner is a Protestant."*

It's a charming anecdote. It involves dealing with right/wrong … and some contingencies, e.g., what if Dick didn't wear a clerical collar?

Just. Justice is a popular topic as our society deals with more-than-enough legal requirements and proscriptions. It is not a new topic; we can trace the concern for justice well back in Judeo-Christian tradition.

Abraham: Justice is part of *covenant* expectations: people walked with God in a spirit of trust. Paul notes Abraham's faith counted as rightness – a sign of creator-creature bonding.

David: One thousand years pass; Israel is a more structured and complex society. Covenant experience aligns more with religious than civic institutions. Justice codified human law, perhaps with some reference to covenant trust. King David suggests this connection in his last words to his people (2 Sam 22:3b): *"He who rules over men must be just, ruling in the fear of God."*

David's phrase, *the fear of God* is expected to affect justice. The shading of God-based *rightness* is a qualifying factor:

Justice (general)	Rightness (personal)
Safeguards social interactions	A measure for individual behaviors
Concern: common protection	Concern: mercy, generosity, kindness
Upholds an impersonal standard	Biased to favor the deprived

Amos: Two hundred fifty years after David. Israel's social ordering is fragmented. Civil and religious matters/institutions are separated. Each has its own modes to enforce rules and social expectations:

- City gate magistrates: charged to set right secular, civil violations.
- Temple/priesthood: authority to sustain spiritual/moral rightness/duties.

Amos' (5:24) "test" highlights familiar social issues: fair, equitable, just.

Fair. After I began school, a second sister joined the family, so I grew up with one brother and two sisters. Our home was an arena for lively contests about "fairness" – with things, with opportunities. We each defined our own measure for favoritism: Our self-identity was the norm to assess/check favoritism.

We grew to accept a norm other than self. Our personal understanding drew on parental guidance, personal experience, social and religious values. This broader measure modified competitive and selfish drives. We learned what is fair: conscience, an inner sense of right as a valid norm.

Equitable. (Alas, the unequal is generally more obvious!) Phillip was repeating eighth grade with us; he was learning-challenged. Mrs. Johnson, the teacher, helped us make Phillip feel accepted as part of the class. She never allowed patronizing interactions. Phillip shared in every learning unit and class activity.

Phillip didn't advance when the class was promoted to ninth grade. However, those of us moving on from Mrs. Johnson's class-family owned a clearer sense of what is equitable: behavior which assures social acceptance and inclusiveness.

Life-lesson learning happens best in a belonging, covenant body – any group sharing values and refining them in daily practice. Christians do this whenever a gathering of two-three (or a hundred) meet in Christ's name.

In such a gathering, our behavior (being) takes precedence over agenda (doing). Our sharing and actions are influenced by an inner sense of right. Interdependence has precedence over autonomy/independence. Justice and righteousness remain definable, but wholeness is their common check.

The prophet Amos mourned that secularized order rejected covenant belonging and divorced justice from righteousness. This touched on life-choices deeper than church-state separation. (The entire prophetic tradition considered them complementary!) The prophets' cries observed that Israel increasingly loosed itself from spiritual ties. The prophets' laments consistently connected to promises of God-based hope and expectation. Faith seemed fast fading; covenant promise more distant … and in time the nation is exiled!

One wintry night, Jesus rests in a manger – beginning this human experience. In his ministry, Jesus repeatedly tempers justice with rightness – inside the Temple, outside the city gates. This sparks clashes with both civil rulers and religious leaders.

The Sadducees manipulated secular justice and sacred righteousness to appear like a State matter. Jewish leaders got what they wanted; Pilate acquiesced. With the resurrection God reclaims, redeems, the tie of justice and rightness. The Holy Spirit emboldens the Church to maintain God's covenant standard in history.

In Jesus' teaching/actions righteousness merges intrinsically with justice. Rightness is loosed from holy boxes kept inside holy spaces, e.g., arks, temples, church buildings, etc. Rightness colors justice in human encounters both expected and strange. It flows like streams, falling waters – Amos' verbs give justice and rightness life, continually refining, purifying.

The Pharisees once ask Jesus to confirm the rightness of stoning an adulterous woman. She violated a law written on a scroll, kept in a box, stored in another safe place (the Temple). Jesus' response: A sinless stone-thrower is a prerequisite for this "justice" demanded by the Pharisees. Alas, the Pharisees had none handy. Here it is: rightness infuses law with mercy, forgiveness, equity. Justice is not loss, but restoration of self-value, identity, acceptance – horizontally and vertically!

Modern culture strongly endorses personal rights; subtly, persons become self-absorbed – tied up in self, my losses/my gains. Easily we identify with the young lawyer's request for Jesus to guarantee his place in eternal life (Luke 10:25ff). Jesus asks the person to share his ideas: The lawyer offers a printout inventory of religious "do's." Jesus says it is not enough. Yes, do what is written; **also** be engaged in covenant caring. The lawyer leaves in sadness, preferring unattached self-rightness. So I give examples of these qualities:

Just: Mr. Jones, the corner storekeeper when I was a child, always broke crackers from the barrel into the crumbs required to meet the exact weight requested: "no more/no less." The action was just; it lacked rightness.

Fair: A Brahman stood on the sidelines following a road accident in New Delhi. He safeguarded his ritual purity by raucously ordering others to help an injured cyclist. (Ironically, another Brahman risked the touch of mercy with his own offer of help ... <u>un</u>separation of sacred and secular).

<u>Equitable</u>: In the 1990s, New Delhi's new Apollo hospital set a healthy surcharge for patients with adequate income to offset costs of treatment and care for the poor.

Justice and rightness bond in sacramental union, a human witness of God-with-us. God's stewards honor this in all dealings – however small/large our circle of action, our circle of influence.

It is a blessing to gather with seniors who keep justice and rightness firmly linked. They share the joy of purposefully removing barriers (or antagonism) between legality and morality. They witness to love that seals a commitment to be just **and** right. It is a holy alternative to moral/ethical manipulation ... the contrivance sadly exercised at Calvary.

When the government of India honored Mother Teresa with its Nehru Prize, she addressed the assembled members of Parliament, President, Supreme Court Justices. The citation was read; it listed her services to the poor, elaborately detailing acts of mercy and charity for the unwanted and unneeded. In her acceptance remarks, she referred to the citation and added the part grace has in all her service. With her usual gentleness, she quietly said: "I know what I am doing for the poor. The question is: 'What are you doing for the poor?'"

She shared with the government her own inner law, unlegislated benefits of grace ... options to include rightness with justice for all.

Meditation Twenty-Four

"Jesus loves me, this I know" – but that's drivel if we miss the implicit subtext:
"Jesus gives me power-in-love, this I know!"
A senior faces a critical decision: Will I continue to cherish both Jesus' love
and Jesus' power? Can't I use the love and retire from bearing the power?
Jesus doesn't knock, leave a secret pal love basket, then scurry off.
He knocks; he waits.
Don't pretend you're not there! Let him in!
Draw on your living faith and answer the knock –
let yourself share what the encounter initiates.
Accept or reject! It's everyone's life-and-death authority.
Jesus writes your song of love – so sing it!

An Authority of One – Me

When Jesus had come down from the mountain, great crowds followed him; and there was a leper who came and knelt before him, saying, "Lord, if you choose, you can make me clean." Jesus stretched out his hand and touched him, saying, "I do choose. Be made clean." Immediately his leprosy was cleansed. Then Jesus said to him, "See that you say nothing to anyone; but go show yourself to the priest, and offer the gift that Moses commanded, as a testimony to them."

When he entered Capernaum, a centurion came to him with an appeal: "Lord, my servant is lying at home paralyzed, in terrible distress." And Jesus said to him, "I will come and cure him." The centurion answered, "I am not worthy to have you come under my roof; but only speak the word, and my servant will be healed. For I also am a man under authority, with soldiers under me; and I say to one, 'Go,' and he goes, and to another, 'Come,' and he comes, and to my slave, 'Do this,' and the slave does it."

When Jesus heard him, he was amazed and said to those gathered, "Truly I tell you, in no one in Israel have I found such faith. I tell you, many will come from east and west and will eat with Abraham and Isaac and Jacob in the kingdom of heaven, while the heirs of the kingdom will be thrown into the outer darkness, where there will be weeping and gnashing of teeth."

And to the centurion Jesus said, "Go; let it be done for you according to your faith." And the servant was healed in that hour.　　　　　　(Matthew 8:1-13)

Judy Garland sang *"But Not for Me"* in George Gershwin's stage/film musical *Girl Crazy*:

They're singing songs of love, but not for me;
A lucky star's above, but not for me...

It laments a personal expectation, even a yearning – sadly, one not realized.

The reading from Matthew depicts events after Jesus' Sermon on the Mount. It drew a large crowd on that hillside near Capernaum; the peoples' curiosity whetted by reports of this new-style teacher. Jesus speaks with authority about belonging in community. His insights are crystal-clear; he illustrates them with radical examples.

Jesus uses the inclusive "you" throughout the Sermon. It conveys every person is part of the community. He speaks of real relationships: each with ongoing connections. His Sermon illustrates how one's actions link both to creator and neighbor: expressions of love make bonds of caring, sharing.

Some on this hillside may feel like outsiders, on Israel's fringes. Some cling to long-practiced defenses of independence or secretly borne hurts. They identify with the refrain: *He speaks words of love, but not for me!*

Jesus comes down to the plain, the entourage aglow with joyous expectation. There waits a leper with more than enough weakness and guilt and loneliness and anxiety and despair. Perhaps, stirred by the crowd's enthusiasm, he ventures a cry for attention. He gets what he asks for, <u>and</u> something more. He encounters what becomes part of the scandal of the Gospel: grace is free, but not private. Its lifeline is holy fellowship.

The leper accepts Jesus' <u>competence</u> (ability) to heal: ...you can heal my body! But the leper has little <u>confidence</u> (trust, faith) Jesus is willing to heal – he qualifies his request with: *if you want to!* The leper identifies himself narrowly – a loner. That's his trip-up. He misses a key factor: faith rises from communion. It connects your confidence with Jesus' competence.

That kind of communion puzzled Israel; it's a dilemma for many modern Christians. We resist forces tampering with an independent self. Consider the range of leverage skills used to lobby in the courts of the Almighty, pressing God to <u>will</u> things He <u>might</u> do for us. We're like the leper: It is deeply upsetting to make public our search for a private fount of blessing.

This happens easily. Recall the psalmist's query, wondering if out in the starry heavens a Being <u>is</u> mindful of self (Psalm 8:4). It is the nonbelievers' question: *"If your God is almighty, is He good?"* And our brave reply: *"O yes, God so cares for the world...!"* God *can* if only God *will* – the scandal that looks like <u>powerless love</u> ... or, is it <u>loveless power</u>?

This dilemma colors Israel's historic identity: the <u>chosen</u> nation repeatedly loses its selfhood – to Egypt, Assyria, Babylon, Rome! (Why doesn't an omnipotent Lord safeguard national identity?) Israel observes Jesus cares, and might claim some divine connection, but this isn't what Israel expected. He questions their ideas about what is "righteous" and "unrighteous." He dwells on love. These Jews are puzzled by the thought of coating power in love.

Eventually Jesus faces stark, unabashed earth power in league with Roman authority. They nail him to a cross, then challenge him to use the power he claims for himself. Alas, say passing observers, he *"saves"* others but not himself!

Indeed, if power and love are in conflict, then we've got to claim love and trust power is its consequence – beyond our control. Was the leper up to that? Are we? Is that the friend we want in Jesus? The New Testament is all about affirming God's promise to Isaiah (65:17,24): *"I am creating new. Before people call out, I'll answer; before they finish speaking, I'll have heard."* Love gives form to power, not the other way round! Jesus reveals this. Listen. Asked why he bothered with sinners, he told three stories:

- A shepherd seeks a sheep who nibbled its way out of sight without meaning to be isolated.
- A necklace coin can only rest where it falls; the owner fixes on recovery because the coin's part in the whole surpasses its single face value.
- A son rehearsing his remorse abruptly feels a father's embrace, and a kiss mutes the boy's memorized speech; the father whispers: *My child!* – like a song of love written just for the son.

Bethlehem to Calvary and all the dusty miles between simply do not add up to power alone as redemptive. They add up to anguish in God's heart with its marks still on the hands and feet.

Bethlehem to Calvary and all the dusty miles between mean God's access to the human heart is only by yielding self to God, to others. Quarrels do not stop until we are ready to stop them. People are not made good if they do not want to. The prayer phrase *"thy will be done"* isn't about God's ability, but our readiness.

What bemused the leper – and us: God's restraint, not his power. God's concern for persons is their wholeness, completeness. That makes faith a renewing adventure different from sanitizing bad parts with spiritual antibiotics.

That's the leper's difficulty: He wants to put it all on Jesus. Hear him: *If you want to, you can heal my body.* Listen carefully or you miss the scandal. Jesus says, *"I want to,"* then passes the action back to the leper, *"Be clean."* Note what Jesus implies: *"Be what you aren't now ... let this love affect your domain of self!"* Again and again, Jesus asks (in many forms): Are you ready to accept prayer-answers fully? The situation seems to move from power lacking love to love appearing to lack power ... and never is! It's called redemption; it was demonstrated on a cross and with an empty tomb. Self-preservation matters so much to us; what matters to God is gathering the lost in community.

After Jesus' encounter with the leper, Matthew tells of Jesus' response to the Roman captain's request to heal a subordinate. The captain apologizes for his boldness. But catch what Jesus observes: The captain trusts connections that convey power. (This "flow" is inherent in a military chain of command.) Connection keeps authority's power effective. The captain's trust assures Jesus' power will be effective. Jesus uses this faith as a model, a seed of promise. He stands it against the landscape filled with weeds and tares of a spiritually timid, doubting, cautious Israel – too frightened to harvest the benefits.

It is not easy for faith to fashion this kind of love. So often this love can do little about life's hazards without ceasing to be love. That calls for confidence (faith) to risk outcomes beyond earth-fixed checks and balances. Without that confidence, it ceases to be power true to itself!

This is Job's amazing discovery – peeling away a layer of private bitterness to expose himself to God's revitalizing compassion. Job's hurt meant giving up his neatly defined "god" and risk exploration of/with a caring Lord (Job 42). *"I admit I once lived by rumors of you, Lord; now I have it all firsthand – in my own experience!"* It was so much more than getting answers! Not loveless power, nor powerless love. It is a new equation of the nouns: power in love!

Look at Peter's biography: erratic attempts to serve without yielding self-control, spiritual reins! Peter: self-determination battling self-sacrifice!

- *"Depart from me … I'm a sinner."* Jesus answers: *"Follow me."*
- *"You will never clean my feet!"* Jesus' response: *"All or nothing."*
- *"I will never deny you."* The cock crowed the third time.
- *"Do you love me?" "You know I love you." "Show it in charity."*
- *"Quo vadis?"* ("Where are you going?), as Peter ran down the Appian Way to avoid personal persecution.

Finally, the fisherman heard the Lord's song of love – just for Peter!

The Word is Incarnate, with us, full of grace and truth. Power – love: eternally available. One redeems, one reforms … neither rivaling for primacy or dominance. Like a potter's hands supporting malleable material until the clay has confidence it is a right, pleasing, soul-housing vessel.

It is not an easy Gospel. On the hillside, the Word goes out to the crowd, but its effect always begins in an audience of one: *"Behold, I stand at the door and knock; if you* (<u>singular</u> now) *hear and open…"* (Rev 3:20). You do it, of course, at your peril. You fix your eye on the lodestar, one risen and returned as Spirit. The outcome is a shared journey *en route* to waiting glory.

Meditation Twenty-Five

"Holy" is a term we use cautiously – it suggests separateness.
Scripture considers it an essential Christian quality: a motive to serve others.
History praises those acclaimed for extraordinary holiness.
Is there such a thing as "ordinary" holiness? Of course.
Seniors easily share unexceptional holiness – holiness without a halo.
It is a behavior refined by a commitment to be right and loving.
Seniors' maturity makes it easier to let acts of love happen!
In the time left, it is good for seniors to share unceremonious holiness,
it's a great antidote for skepticism and detachment.

Un-exceptional Holiness

A Pharisee asked Jesus to eat with him, so he went into the Pharisee's house and took his place at the table. A woman in the city, who was a sinner, learned that Jesus was eating in the Pharisee's house. She brought an alabaster jar of ointment, came to Jesus and began to bathe his feet with her tears and dry them with her hair. She continued kissing his feet and anointing them with the ointment.
Now when the host Pharisee saw it, he said to himself, "If this man were a prophet, he would know what kind of woman touches him – a sinner." Jesus spoke up and said, "Simon, I have something to say to you. A certain creditor had 2 debtors: one owed 500 denarii, the other 50. When they could not pay, he canceled both debts. Now which of them will love him more?" Simon answered, "I suppose the one whose greater debt was canceled." And Jesus said, "You judge rightly."
Then turning toward the woman, he said to Simon, "Look at this woman. I entered your house; you gave me no water for my feet, but she bathed my feet with her tears and dried them with her hair. You gave me no kiss of greeting, but from the time I came in she has not stopped kissing my feet. You did not anoint my head with oil, but she anointed my feet with ointment. Therefore I tell you, her sins, which were many, have been forgiven; hence she shows great love. But the one to whom little is forgiven, loves little." Then Jesus said to her, "Your sins are forgiven." Others at the table muttered, "Who is this who even forgives sins?" And Jesus said to the woman, "Your faith has saved you, go in peace." (Luke 7:36-50)

Personal behaviors help or hinder relationships. Behaviors make the inner spirit visible. Actions reveal our defining qualities. Actions energize (or weaken) interpersonal connections. Others' behaviors affect us: some are life-*lifting,* some are life-*limiting!*

Behaviors gauge the values we treasure in our souls. We discern how others affect us and *vice versa.* Early in life, a person's habits reveal an inner spirit. Good habits bring social acceptance, respect. Bad habits may bring rejection, detachment. A person's inner spirit is vulnerable. It produces fruits, outcomes – expected and unexpected.

During my early, preschool years, I remember people saying: *"The Dickey-Bird is watching!"* – observing what I let influence me, watching me make good or bad choices. We sang about these before Christmas:

> *You better watch out, you better not cry,*
> *You better not pout, I'm telling you why!*
> *Santa Claus is coming to town.*
> *He knows when you've been bad/good, so be good....*

Early development helps a child make choices that are personally and socially healthy. The idea of being "good" or "less good" involves others. With each birthday, a person's private world expands; we adapt to others' expectations. These impact shared joy and goodwill.

When I was 5, my pastor-father was given a new appointment. On moving day, we reached the new parsonage. It was alive with cheerful hospitality. A host of women welcomed us warmly. This new space was filled with demonstrations of loving Spirit-gifts. ("Hospitality" has origins in the Greek term *philoxenia,* "lover of strangers").

Three years later we had another move. We arrived at noon on a rainy autumn day. The large parsonage seemed unloved, lifeless – bathed in grayness inside and out. The symbolic "welcome" was a scribbled note: "Cold-cuts in the refrigerator. Help yourself." A do-it-yourself welcome! The atmosphere was eerily Halloween-like: we felt abandoned to the hospitality of ghostly spirits. The first local human initiative came after two days: at 8 a.m., a lady rang the bell, offered a bowl of Jell-o, and retreated hastily to her car (its motor left running!).

Hospitality is a skill that connects us with others. We learn it, we practice it, we refine it. It generates behaviors that establish and enhance friendly connections. It is a foundation for fellowship, the gift of an indwelling Spirit.

Shortly before retirement, the Naga people (an ancient tribal culture in northeast India) invited me to speak for celebrations honoring Baptist mission work begun 100 years earlier. A welcoming party received me at the provincial airport; we began a five-hour Jeep ride to the site deep in the Himalayas. After three hours on mountain roads, we stopped and entered a small residence.

Our halt was not scheduled, but the woman of the house recognized our welcoming party. Prepared cold food was carried in from the Jeep. In silence, she left the room and returned with hot rice, then left. Every Naga home keeps provision ready; unannounced visitors in this desolate area may need hospitality.

In God's household, hospitality is a fruit of holiness. It is shared whenever two-three meet and share bonding with Christ. We find two patterns: 1) Exceptional holiness, e.g., Mother Teresa, who embodied and shared God's self-giving love to "make the wounded whole."; 2) **un**exceptional holiness, rarely dramatic but always a spirit-influence to show value and make care visible!

Hospitality: actions that break down separation and ensure acceptance! It demonstrates behaviors that:
- Welcome fruits of grace – redemption and release.
- Honor human worth – fellowship's safety net amid shifts/changes.
- Extend the household's circle – with wideness of mercy.

The Upper Room experience includes two events: the institution of the Lord's Supper (bread and wine); and Jesus' foot-washing (basin and towel). The latter reveals and confirms a new Spirit-protocol!

Foot-washing recreates and reforms hospitality – it has sacramental overtones. And we may interject hastily: "How?" The action is service. This ministry cuts through unright protocols – unholy reminders that taint relationships. Cleansing (given, received!) orients service into grace. A fresh air comes into the atmosphere, as suggested in this verse:

There's a sweet, sweet Spirit in this place,
and I know that it's the Spirit of the Lord;
without a doubt we'll know,
that we have been revived when we shall leave this place.

In Eastern cultures – still in rural Indian settings – a guest's arrival halts routine activity. It marks an intentional break, a valued discontinuity –

a time for "exchange." The host/hostess now serves. The focus is to honor and be honored. In many places, the first act is foot-washing, hand-washing. It rinses away road dust; it refreshes physically. It is a holy gesture – a blessing given, a blessing received. Symbolically, social separations are absent for this time and place.

In Luke 7, Jesus teaches and heals in Galilee. He brings to life the widow of Nain's dead son. In another village, a senior Pharisee, Simon, invites Jesus to his home for a meal. (This is not exceptional; a visiting spiritual personality is always so entertained.) In the East, such village events are always "open." As invited guests gather in the host's courtyard for the meal, curious villagers enter and move about freely – a milling crowd is not unusual. However, here the host disregards standard hospitality: greeting and foot-washing. (There is no explanation. Perhaps the host tests protocols … an unspoken question about Jesus' spiritual standing – after all, Jesus persists with an unconventional commentary on the law!) Invitees take their places; the food is served. A local "sinful" woman notices the neglected hospitality. Without comment she washes the visitor's feet with tears, dries them with her hair. Simon sees this and utters an aside: *"Shouldn't a prophet know this is contact with a sinner?"* Jesus condones the sinner's act; he doesn't condemn the sinner. Again Jesus reinterprets law-protocol in the light of grace-protocol. Jesus narrates a story about persons with differing debts who are forgiven equally, not proportionally. The focus shifts: from debtor to creditor, from obligation to generosity, from sinner to Lord, from law to grace.

This posits another New Testament subtlety – a contrast of two labels for "sinner.": 1) debtor: one who keeps the law but avoids loving initiatives; and 2) trespasser: one whose unright behaviors cause division or separation.

Without fanfare, Jesus connects his coming (Incarnation) with his ministry of grace (Atonement). (As in the core good news in John 3:16). Note the two connections in this text: 1) Jesus forgives sin: God's covenant love (Incarnation); and 2) Simon's challenge: unrightness of physical contact, the cost of reconciliation (Atonement). The practice of law encounters the protocol of grace.

The Atonement benefits both debtor and trespasser: ransomed, healed, restored, forgiven.

Jesus unites service and holiness as hospitality – an outer form of inner spirituality. Paul addresses this often when helping early churches shape a social model of life inside **and** outside God's household.

154

One furlough, a United Methodist Women's group invited us to its small church in rural Michigan. After a brief introduction, we spoke about India to a polite, almost impassive, audience. Then all were directed to the fellowship hall for refreshments. Silently, the women watched Sylvia and me take our bit of <u>every</u> item, then sit. Still silent, they surrounded us. We tasted something, made appreciative sounds – suddenly, a burst of effusive glee and conversation. We <u>received</u> with appreciation their personal initiatives of welcome. It opened a floodgate of bonding warmth. Perhaps if that gesture of and response to "hospitality" happened at the beginning, we would connect swiftly in spirit and mission!

The Upper Room hospitality (John 13) is mystery. And it is a model for the journey of holy people. The basin/towel gesture rids formal impediments to fellowship. It cleanses, readies us to receive and share the holiness of Christ-in-us. Such spiritual behavior is never **of** the world, but always viable **in** the world.

This is <u>un</u>exceptional holiness. It's an essential quality for ordinary interactions. This protocol carries wondrous benefits of mercy:

- Always soothes, never startles.
- Always inclusive, never selective.
- Always the offer of grace, never without risk.

<u>Un</u>exceptional holiness: hospitality. It is a Christian protocol that shows faith energizing love – even when entertaining unannounced angels!

Meditation Twenty-Six

Prayer is a love duet; it celebrates communion.
It bonds the Master with a steward of grace and service.
It is the same Master who calls you, commissions you, empowers you.
(Remember: since your last time together the Master is active …
engaging with others in his stewards' cadre!)
In prayer we clarify commitments and resources to
further the Spirit's purposes.
In prayer we are comforted, restored, refreshed.
In prayer we feel the rhythms of grace and hear echoes of rejoicing:
"You did it to the least….."

Take in the Extravagant Dimensions of Christ's Love

Everyone, then, is living in pure grace – God's immeasurable goodness. And it is important that you do not misinterpret yourselves as people who are bringing this goodness to God. No, God brings it all to you. The only accurate way to understand ourselves is by what God is and by what he does for us, not by what we are and what we do for him. (Romans 12:3)
I ask the Father to strengthen you by his Spirit … that Christ will live in you as you open the door and invite him in … that you will be able to take in the extravagant dimensions of Christ's love … Live full lives, full in the fullness of God. (Ephesians 3:16-17, Peterson)

Ronald Reagan – in his seventies - addressed University of California students. One student said it was impossible for Reagan's generation to understand the then-middle-aged boomer and younger generations:

Student: *You grew up in a different world. Today we have television, jet travel, space ventures, nuclear energy, computers.*

Reagan: *You're right. We didn't have those things when we were young. We invented them.*

The student presumed new results are most important. Reagan didn't deny this, but he rooted "value" in vision, inspiration, possibilities.

Each year my preacher-family faced the possibility of "a move." For many years, Conference appointments were made in September; moves took place about the fourth week in a new school year ... very unsettling for children. Preacher's kids acquire skills to survive a need to face new situations. Lifestyle changes are inconvenient but need not diminish creative options.

Paul challenges Ephesian Christians to connect with the Spirit to *"live full lives."* This *fullness* is not bits we accumulate. No, Paul expands an idea written in Romans: *"God brings it all to you."*

Prayer life – for Paul – is a wanted child communing with an attentive parent. It is more than texting spiritual updates. Prayer interaction opens the way for blessing/fullness. It is a risk; it raises a caution. Awareness that comes to us in prayer may threaten our autonomy and independence. It might link to a direct call: *"Deny self ... take up the cross."*

A *Hagar the Horrible* comic strip illustrates prayer as a two-way experience. Hagar sits at the dining room table devouring food; Helga – his wife – calls from the kitchen.

Helga: *Did you say grace?*

(Hagar keeps chewing, raises his eyes heavenward, mumbling something.)

Voice (from above): *Don't talk with your mouth full!*

How easily we pray with our "mouth full" – perhaps overly filled with ourselves!

A senior's vital spiritual discipline: Review prayer habits regularly. A good opening question: Is my prayer too full, too weighted, with unedited messages? Does my "mouth full" distract from healthful communion? Does it strain the power connection between God's initiatives and how faith molds my actions?

A good prayer is not overloaded with crises! That requires us to sort, set aside some tendencies to ventilate each and every worry we face. If we fill prayers with less of ourselves, we are open to greater vision, energizing inspiration. Here are some guidelines:

1) Permit yourself to: a) evaluate concerns, and b) test aptness of elements in a prayer. The Spirit inspires with solutions for real issues.

2) Infuse fresh leaven when prayer patterns go flat. Spiritual refreshment includes repentance ... get beyond the present mindset.

3) "Cleanse" prayer issues (like cleaning blurred lenses). Allow for new insights – beyond unevaluated guessing and tired clichés.

4) Increase spiritual goals so prayer gets new form and shading. Adoration, confession, thanksgiving, supplication/intercession need not always be symmetrical and equal. Content need not be too gray. Keep your approach fresh; prepare **and** perform private prayer well.

Prayer-communion is an Emmaus Road time with the Spirit – a journey with discovery and revelation. Life circumstances change; we enter new environments. In such uncertainty, we can pray: "Thank you, God, for your goodness; prepare me for inspiration." (Perhaps this is Jesus' intention when he prays: *"Let this cup pass from me ... but thy will be done."*)

Inspiration lessens an urge to be in control. It may lead the activist part of us to different service – beside stiller waters and greener pastures! Or, the passive part of us may be drawn to service in the swirling rapids!

Evening shadows fall; a youngster kneels by the bedside – hands in prayer-mode, eyes uplifted, open. There is a litany of concerns for family, friends, pets, teachers – even minor shortcomings. Then: "And now, God, tell me – what can I do for you?"

Some might think the child expected a reply of information. I suspect the child was ready for inspiration. Prayer with pauses and spaces offers amazing scope for this. Wait, listen! As Paul says to Ephesian colleagues: *"God works gently within you"* – an Emmaus Road partner in your life-journey and service.

Prayer alters how we view ourselves in the space where we spend time/activity. Gently, God helps us see joy and service often glossed over in rapidly changing conditions. God may even inspire someone else to action in response to our petitions.

A real benefit of prayer is communion. God dwells deeply in the spirit of the one praying. Prayer imperceptibly shows us new subtleties of fellowship.

Cindy, her first year away at college, experienced the mix of independence <u>and</u> separateness from close family ties. It is a Friday evening. She responds to the knock on her dorm-room door; it's her brother Peter.

> Cindy: *Peter! What are you doing here?*
> Peter: *I heard your message on the answering machine at home ... anxiety about next week's math exam. I thought I could help.*
> Cindy: *Peter, I know you're good at math, but this isn't like your high school class!*
> Peter: *I know, but I'm taking some college-level calculus now.* (During that weekend Peter and Cindy identified ways to achieve good results. Peter prepared to leave; Cindy was teary.)
> Peter: *What's wrong?*
> Cindy: *I just realized right now how much you mean to me.*
> Peter: *No. You just found out how much <u>you</u> mean to <u>me</u>.*

In prayer, be ready to sense the Lord's voice saying something like this: "*Open yourself to take in the extravagant dimension of my love ... We can do anything you know!*"

In such communion, perhaps for the first time, you know how much you mean to God! No senior is ever relegated to a no-longer-active roster of God's stewards. Make certain your prayer time includes room/accommodation to listen. Prayer time is together time. The communication brings the redemptive power of God's initiatives to keep your faith purposeful, effective.

Listen. God does – fully, intentionally, without prejudgment. God intends your life to experience the Father's own completeness. Listen. God never speaks to you with his mouth full!

Meditation Twenty-Seven

For Paul, "the peace of God" restores missing harmonies.
(Most earth-peace endeavors are content to modify conflicts.)
Paul then rearranges the words, a new phrase: "the God of peace."
This dynamic engages us in the benefit of covenant communion.
Seniors find the Lord's peace affects real transitions and cherished expectations.
Seniors refine the skills of love – time is short, they want loving actions to be productive, less vague.
Seniors share the "the peace of God/the God of peace" less blithely, more generously.
Fruits of the Spirit are blessings to distribute, not bounty to live on!

Peace of GOD of Peace

It's wonderful what happens when Christ displaces worry at the center of your life [i.e., <u>the peace of God</u>]. Summing it all up, friends, I'd say you'll do best by filling your minds and meditating on things true, noble, reputable, authentic, compelling, gracious – the best, not the worst; the beautiful, not the ugly; things to praise, not things to curse ... and God, who makes everything work together, will work you into his most excellent harmonies [i.e., <u>the God of peace</u>].

(Philippians 4:7b-9, Peterson)

Creation's sixth day – dawn. God says: "*Let us make the human being in our image.*" It is so. God observes this is *"very good,"* i.e., what God intends.

Today – dawn. My wife and I take our regimen of medications and supplements. This sustains our physical well-being – doing this regularly is very good. Supplements are a good resolution for defined needs.

Psalm 42 opens with a lament: *As a deer longs for flowing streams, so longs my soul for you, O God.* The psalmist identifies the need:

- Explicit – a deer seeks water to quench physical thirst.

- Implicit – a psalmist seeks fellowship to satisfy spirit-longing. *My soul longs for you, O God,* identifies a real heart-hunger.

The psalmist faces taunts from persons who mock a spiritual need as irrelevant, fanciful, unreal. Those who jeer settle for earth-bound conditions and man-made solutions. They sneer at the idea of a beyond-earth dimension: "*Where is your God?*" Two-dimensional life on our horizontal plane is enough for them. The psalmist relies on God's vertical dimension in this human experience we label "real life".

We recall Teilhard de Chardin's description of our Christian identity: We are not human beings having a spiritual experience, we are spiritual beings having a human experience. He reprioritizes the link of horizontal and vertical planes – faith-perfected reality intersects with earth's reality:

- earthly well-being is the absence of woes.

- spiritual well-being is wholeness.

Saul's Damascus Road encounter is the iconic model of a human adopting de Chardin's affirmation. Paul describes his life after this event as being *in Christ*. Saul the human being (self-as-self) is now Paul the spiritual being (self-in-Christ). He experiences transforming grace – God's serenity replaces self-driven zeal. As Paul, he perceives self differently; the peace of God reconstitutes the human experience. It clears a channel for grace in place of Saul's torrential flow of zeal.

A spiritual being has new priorities for the human experience. Life continues **in** our world, but not just **of** the world. Grace reinterprets both law and morality. Our human experience lifeline links to Christ as the head. Thus, *in Christ*, the human is a steward of grace – a gift that offers wholeness.

Hindu persons often came to our New Delhi church as inquirers. Most regularly observed prescribed Hindu rites – as a dutiful channel for spiritual assurance. (Like Nicodemus, they presume life-experience disconnects from spirit truth.) They came trying to deal with persistent heart-hungers. Many found Christian faith resolves this. It brings serenity of spirit and joy in fellowship. The new life gift is inner-outer harmony; self-striving yields to belonging, sharing.

In Philippians 4:4ff Paul praises this experience of being found and belonging: *Celebrate God all day, every day!* Paul goes on: *Before you know it, a sense of God's wholeness, everything coming together for good, will come and settle you down. It's wonderful what happens when Christ displaces worry at the center of our life.*

Paul calls this the peace of God – a divine gift and magnificent stability inherent for any spiritual being.

The peace of God is a gift with "strings attached"! It is phantom until a person lets peace leaven personal, ongoing human experience. (This is the stewardship factor.) Paul clarifies this with the complementary phrase, the God of peace. *Christ-in-me* begins a blessing. My stewardship shares the blessing, assures continuity. Visualize this in terms of our human physiology:
a) *Christ-in-me* provides stabilizing bones/sinew for my spiritual being; and
b) *in Christ* I garner drive and nerve for action, initiative that affects others' human experience.

A spiritual being has an array of new qualities *"filling the mind."* ("Mind" – the English translation of Paul's Greek word implies a blend of right sense, right attitude, right action.) Paul often notes this dynamic of self with Christ: *Let your mind be transformed ...; have this mind in you that was in Christ Jesus; fill your minds.* Paul found life *in Christ* exhilarating; he waxes lyrically on its options. *Meditate on things true, noble, reputable, authentic, compelling, gracious – the best, not the worst; the beautiful, not the ugly; things to praise, not things to curse.* This peace of God makes each Christian a spiritual reservoir of redeeming leaven **in** the world.

Families in India with mentally challenged children/youths generally shield them from public exposure. This motivated a woman parishioner to ask Sylvia to form and develop a community outreach program. Its intention: to redeem the shaded human experience of these children/families. Carefully planned, the program dealt with major obstacles to achieve noble, compelling outcomes:

1) Generate positive self-awareness and value in the children/youths.
2) Raise esteem in families as program participants develop confidence and skills to socialize and interact.

163

After many months, the public was invited to celebrate fruits of this public service of care/support. Scores of challenged children and youths – costumed as quadrupeds, fish, and birds – excitedly and boldly acted out Saint-Saens' *Carnival of the Animals*. The American International School orchestra performed the music. Public response was grand! Parents and guests raised cheers it *could* be possible ... and released tears for fears it could *never* be.

The outcome: Participants encountered their spiritual beings and saw it affect their human experience! The <u>God of peace</u> empowered the program staff's input to restore, redeem. Paul affirms this: *God, who makes everything work together, will work you into his most excellent harmonies.*

What accomplishes such noble, compelling goals? Persons of faith know sharing spiritual gifts and graces is a balm for the obvious pain borne by any whose human experience is less than whole.

<u>Peace of God:</u> A balm of grace soothes, heals inflammatory distractions.

<u>God of peace:</u> Engages servants' energy to redeem human brokenness. *Rejoice in the Lord, always! I can do all things through him who strengthens me. ... Celebrate God all day! Whatever I have, wherever I am, I can make it through anything in the One who makes me who I am.* (Phil 4:4, 12-13, Peterson)

This may be especially touching for us seniors who yearn for peace that calms the ever-expanding uncertainty and unrest in our human aging experience. Inner peace is a gift of fellowship with God. (Seniors often defer seeking any "outside" presence – self-reliance is a strong, driving force.)

Trust the benefits attending the gift of the peace of God. Extend that exploration by letting the God of peace use you to share the gift with others distraught by a lack of serenity.

Love Abides

Come to me, all you that are weary and carry heavy burdens, and I will give you rest. Take my yoke upon you, and learn from me; for I am gentle and humble in heart, and you will find rest for your souls. For my yoke is easy, and my burden is light.   (Matthew 11:28-30, NRSV)

Are you tired? Worn out? Burned out on religion? Come to me. Get away with me and you'll receive your life. I'll show you how to take a real rest. Walk with me and work with me – watch how I do it. Learn the unforced rhythms of grace. I won't lay anything heavy or ill-fitting on you. Keep company with me and you'll learn to live freely and lightly.   (Matthew 11:28-30, Peterson)

God created humankind in his <u>image.</u>   (Gen 2:27)

God anticipates fellowship interaction with his human creation – a responder to God's initiatives, a sharer in God's purposes. That is quite different from a static or robotic program. It is God-human activity rising from spiritual bonding.

The Bible calls God's initiative "love" (John 3:16). Its expectation: response – in spirit, in witness. Human response wakens faith. Faith engenders covenant love – love given, love accepted.

Covenant love – perhaps more than any other spiritual experience – brings a unique quality to human relationships. It doesn't happen automatically, it isn't instinctive. It expresses will.

Earlier we noted that life works in two streams. 1) The nature of life (biology with all its intricacies and complexities). 2) The story of life (what we make of life, our biography). Broadly speaking, our nature is given but our story forms from our actions, choices, and opportunities.

Let's return to Genesis' beginnings – two accounts of human creation. The initial account (Gen 1:1-2:3) presents God's intentions and expectations. The subsequent account (Gen 2:4-3:24) describes humans' decisions to deal with choices and conditions. The first affirms human intimacy with God is natural – self is spiritually secure. The second shows humans forming their own history. Too soon our intended nature loses clarity and tangles in confrontations. Human history pioneers in a wilderness of discontinuities. Covenant bonding fades, overtaken by *self*-support.

At retirement, Sylvia and I left India on a Sunday. That morning I conducted worship for an international congregation formed some five years earlier. Before the benediction, elders circled Sylvia and me. Then, on behalf of the congregation, they formally "released" us and affirmed charge of this ministry. We left Delhi that night, the *ministry* carried on. A gentle transition, assuring continuity amid change.

Now I orient faith to who I **am** as a senior. It is an enormous change from an emphasis on what I **do** as a missionary. (Interestingly, one's spiritual fulfillment is less diffused when released from a work/job environment.) However, my senior self is not self-centered. I seek to discern what is relevant outside an institutional framework – a situation with simpler demands but not lacking opportunity. (Read again Jesus' invitation above, Matt 11:28-30.)

This *rest* (release) is not idleness; seniors remain yoked to honor the master's purposes. I am an accountable steward. I uphold the master's expectation and model his qualities. There's a new agenda. The master's rightness (holiness) is less diffused than in a secular workplace. The witness of love is more urgent. This hymn's sentiments celebrate a new level of communion:

> *There is a place of full release, near to the heart of God;*
> *A place where all is joy and peace, near to the heart of God.*
> *O Jesus, blest Redeemer, sent from the heart of God,*
> *Hold us who wait before thee near to the heart of God.*

William Barclay records a legend about Jesus' preministry years. He is a village carpenter specializing in yokes for oxen. He shapes each yoke for its user-animal; this assures comfort and minimizes irritation. The sign outside Jesus' workshop read (in Aramaic): *My Yokes Fit Well*. Perhaps Jesus had that image in mind when he spoke the invitation quoted above.

The word translated "easy" (*chrestos* in Greek) implies the yoke is individually tailored. Specifically, the yoke should not cause pain. Jesus' fuller implication: Bearing God's holiness is grace-full.

Read Matt 11:28-30 in Peterson's translation. **Exploration II** seeks to keep love fresh and energized. Faith leavens and gives savor to our initiatives. Note two challenges for seniors in the passage above. 1) Keep company/walk with Jesus. 2) Ask yourself: Do I, can I, will I live by the *"unforced rhythms of grace"*? Am I a yoked self – with nothing *"heavy or ill-fitting"*? Pause and reflect.

Picture yourself by a seaside, hillside, prairie space, or forest – perhaps in the shade. (It is helpful to be apart, in an environment that is integrated, whole.) Consider this: You want to deal with what is important. Leave the baggage, shun clutter, hold the essentials close. Open yourself to *"learn unforced rhythms of grace."* This is exploration into God. Exploration does not end in seclusion:

> *Just a closer walk with Thee, grant it, Jesus, is my plea,*
> *Daily walking close to Thee, let it be, dear Lord, let it be.*

As you explore be alert, attune senses sharply so you don't miss what comes your way! Seniors are keenly aware we live in a world charged with never-ending urgency. This need not frighten us who move at a different pace.

Urgent and critical are not synonyms. We will not be left behind! Something in every senior's nature and biography sustains the value of self.

Covenant faith redeems time and revalues interdependencies. Seniors are eager to show care, not just be cared for. Seniors generally are sensitive to appropriate care for other seniors, others in like circumstances. This frequently stimulates experiences of true, childlike fellowship … not patronizing and childish pretense.

Gradually my senior understanding refines what real love is about: neither self-gratifying gestures, nor sugary indulgences that lead to diabetes of the soul. Right love soothes both receiver and giver with the *"unforced rhythms of grace"* – verified in shared experiences.

This is bonding love – it connects God's caring (particular, intentional, and straightforward) with God's right (perfected, renewing, sustaining). Our loving actions bring God's values and norms into our history.

A prayer of confession in *The Book of Common Prayer* includes this sentence: *We have left undone those things which we ought to have done, and we have not done those things which we ought to have done, and there is no health in us.* "Health" here draws on an older usage indicating what completes and keeps whole. The confession is a desire to experience again blessings of right and holy living.

Our readiness to generate loving actions and share them is God's seed growing in us … and its fruit. That is part of our faith. Witnessing this faith can be a bit more complicated. Seniors deal with assorted limitations: energy, resources, contacts, readiness for long-term involvements. This does not mean we stop or restrict loving. We do consider new dynamics.

Some are proactive: We reach out with our resources and energies to bring resolution. Some are reactive: We take time to respond.

Eugene Peterson's translation of Deut 6:5 is: *Love God, your God, with all your heart: love him with all that's in you, love him with all you've got!* This is another way to identify the three elements of this new spirit/soul God gives us: mind, heart, might. These integrate and make love right, whole. Peterson's version suggests the Great Commandment keeps us single-minded and wholehearted. Seniors: keep the perspective of ripened faith and spiritual maturity, and respond accordingly – some proactive, some reactive. Peterson aligns *"all that's in you"* and *"all you've got"* to keep your ability in proportion.

I recall a physics lab illustration of integrating what seems different. The topic: Light and Color. The instructor asked: *"What makes up white light?"* No answer. (We knew primary pigment colors: red, yellow, blue – mix these randomly and get a shade of mud!)

Then, in succession, he projected on one spot three primary light colors in succession. First, red; then, green; then, blue. The circle on the screen was pure, brilliant white.

From this, we find a parallel for spirit/soul – integration of right inputs of mind, heart, might. Every expression of spirit-based love needs these three. They don't compete in intensity or ranking. Grace moderates them harmoniously.

The *Meditations* for **Exploration II** address factors in ministries of love. Love is shared intentionally, not randomly. A spiritual being aligns the mind, heart, strength to generate "white" love – the Light of the World!

God the creator breathes life into matter; God the Holy Spirit forms every life *in Christ*. A steward's yoke is purposely fitted. Grace does not patronize; it empowers. It is sacramental – divine affecting human – as the Salisbury *Sacrum Primer (1558)* affirms:

> *God be in my head and in my understanding;*
> *God be in mine eyes, and in my looking;*
> *God be in my mouth, and in my speaking;*
> *God be in my heart, and in my thinking;*
> *God be in mine end, and in my departing.*

Exploration II concludes with the following *Meditation.*

Meditation Twenty-Nine

Old covenant Israel offered sacrifices at Temple worship.
Offerings "atoned" for accrued spiritual shortfall – the imbalance of past
deficiencies and wrongs.
New covenant worship (public, private) works in present/future time.
Present: readiness to be God's good and faithful servers.
Future: spiritual beings maturing for God's call to life beyond death.
Atonement faith accepts God's redeeming grace,
this is why we bear the mark and seal of the cross.
A senior refines faith to de-mystify love and share it generously.

When the Roll Is Called – Down Here

With what shall I come before the Lord, and bow myself before God on high?
Shall I come before him with burnt offerings, with calves a year old? Will the
Lord be pleased with thousands of rams, with ten thousands of rivers of oil?
Shall I give my firstborn for my transgressions, the fruit of my body for the sin
of my soul? (Micah 6:6-7)
He has told you, O mortal, what is good; and what does the Lord require of you
but to do justice, and to love kindness and to walk humbly with our God? (v.8)

171

There's a sweet, sweet Spirit in this place,
and I know that it's the Spirit of the Lord;
there are sweet expressions on each face,
and I know they feel the presence of the Lord.

Those gathered in worship share this praise chorus to celebrate outer and inner serenity. Separations – person-person, person-God – dissolve.

This has not always been so. Some thousand years before Jesus time, pilgrims gathered at the temple in Jerusalem for prayer and sacrifice. Micah has reservations about the intention of those gathering to worship. He suggests it distances them from the Lord whose presence they sought!

Micah (6:6-7) speaks as if he utters a pilgrim's thoughts. *With what shall I stand before the Lord? Shall I come with burnt offerings, thousands of rams, ten thousands of rivers of oil … my firstborn?*

In v.8, the prophet adds his own understanding: *He [God] has told you: and what does the Lord require of you but to do justice, and to love kindness, and to walk humbly with our God.*

When people asked Jesus how to experience God's presence in prayer, he was specific. Don't pray obliquely to a vague, abstract reality. Be forthright in whom you address and what you seek: *Our Father … thy will be done.* Like Micah, Jesus' faith-journey considers prayer communion with God. Permit me to share moments from my faith-journey biography.

It was Tuesday, 6 September 1938, a rural village in southern New Jersey: a church, a primary school, a general store, perhaps a dozen homes at these crossroads leading to outlying farms. My first day in kindergarten finally dawned, and I sat at my little desk. I thrilled to belong in that community of children.

Miss Scott explained the procedures for roll call – each pupil could choose to answer: "Here" or "Present." She read our full name – given and family – beginning with A. We passed L-M-N and neared S. My name was there! I began to understand what it means to <u>be</u> present – to be engaged fully in the life/work of the group, the community, those who belong. More importantly it meant being alert to discovering more about myself – outside my little private world. In my 4-year-old limited capacity I was dealing with Micah's message.

- *Do justice!* Know the norms of what is good and right – and uphold them. One cannot believe rules are good and right unless one commits to the spirit of what is good and right. Belonging (to <u>be</u> present) is how one discovers and shares this.

- *Love kindness (mercy) and forbearance.* Patiently promote what is right. Check how your own skills help good and right happen. I learned it is OK to know what I *desired*. I also learned to recognize that others *deserve* something from me: to belong means others have a claim on me. Again, <u>be</u> present and belong – these goals help me integrate with other selves. I learned a priority: walk with God in order to be humble comfortably.

Life moved beyond kindergarten. I grew in forbearance – a quality that reformed me as circles of belonging expanded. It is easy to do right in familiar comfort zones. Rapid personal development opens new circles of fellowship and involvement – each posing more complex expectations.

Forward to 1945: the challenges of adolescence. A major social challenge: check tendencies of self-rightness, detachment. One tentatively explores the dynamics of being a neighbor – a matter not of geography but of spirit. This takes a self into high-risk territory: show mercy before judging. Gradually, the parable of the Good Samaritan shifts from being a sweet Disneylike film to face-to-face, high-risk involvement. The passing Priest could not allow himself to <u>be</u> present in the situation … nor could the Levite. The outsider Samaritan did.

Fast forward to 1963. The Board of Missions assigned Sylvia and me to serve in India. In consultation with the Indian bishop, a call was recognized: our resumes/orientation assessments comfortably meshed with a real need in New Delhi – establish an urban congregation in the national capital.

Monday, 20 April 1964, 8 p.m. – our train, the Frontier Mail, steamed into Delhi junction. Night had fallen. Amid strange sounds and smells, we strained to sense something familiar – anything! The next day, in the daylight we shift from <u>looking at</u> the place to <u>living in</u> the place. It was unsettling – a world overwhelmingly unfamiliar and different. A question swirls in the mind: *How can I serve the Lord in a strange land?* I visit my treasure of spiritual resources:

- Jesus: *If you want to become my follower, deny self…* Not so easy, because at this moment I am the only reality in my control!
- Paul's directive: *Have this mind in you that was in Christ Jesus … he humbled himself, taking the form of a server …* Yield a claim of self as sufficient.

- God's call to Moses: *Take off your sandals ... you stand on holy ground.* (Ex 3:5) A centuries-old wake-up call when we expand/extend circles of concern: Unfamiliar ground is also holy ground – not for <u>looking</u>, but <u>living</u>.

What does the Lord expect of me, you? Micah, Israel's other prophets, and Jesus condemn injustice – often emotionally. What moves the prophets to make such cries? It is not God's anger, but God's anguish. The anguish is not because laws are broken, but those hurting sense the absence of healing.

Perhaps Jesus' most severe judgments are given in Matthew 25 (the Peterson translation is used here). One illustration uses the common rural practice of sorting sheep and goats. Jesus uses this to indicate the steward's primary quality: love. The King receives into fellowship those designated "sheep" and indicates ways they were *present* with love for others. The King's long litany begins, *I was hungry and you fed me. I was thirsty ... etc.* The chosen didn't remember direct calls for service, and the King says: *Whenever you did one of these things to someone overlooked or ignored, that was me – you did it to me.*

Anyone *in Christ* makes God's love *present*, ready with grace. Divine presence takes up residence in our history. The one named Father bonds with the child, the Head with the body, the Savior with the server, the sacred in the secular. Creation's magnificent intention of interdependence happens. The Lord uses the church to touch the world's hurts and hurting. The Lord <u>is present</u> as healer. Healing is not a change of medication but a change of heart.

We reach our destination, Centenary Methodist Church. Each day exposes us in circles of concern – persons who (for God's sake) deserve us to be *present* ... and for whom we should bring "good news." Much of the "holy ground" was outside the church boundary walls. To <u>be</u> <u>present</u> we had to **go** into <u>their</u> world:

- Be present: provide sewing classes for urban slum women.
- Be present: establish a medical clinic in a refugee shanty town.

We had to be present in order to touch hurts magnified in rapidly changing social conditions. We had to be present with options of forbearance where cultural conditions clashed. We had to be present to make visible and offer God's birthright. (Often God's caring presence seemed stranger to slum-people than our nationality.) We discover "being present" is the most dynamic evangelism in another culture!

Easily – and frequently – anyone can feel God drops us out of mind entirely … we feel forsaken. It is then God most forcefully breaks through the crust of our independence and self-reliance. In those moments of loving forbearance, the Father holds serious conversations with a human soul. Our worst times can be His times. It is a pity not to let Him <u>be present</u> – giving grace, beside lonely footsteps in the sand.

We left India in June 1997. Our feet are no longer on **that** ground – which is still holy, and the Lord's work carries on in the jobs of countless servers. They answer, "Present"! They converse: *"Our Father … thy will be done."*

The mystery of *What does the Lord require of us?* calls us to answer: *Be present!* Our response is not to Micah, but to the Lord. The roll call reverberates across the face of the earth as God calls every spiritual being's name. The reply is heard in the idiom of hundreds of languages and myriad acts of love. It's a surety for the transition to life beyond death.

Exploration III

Hope

As a child, "hope" related to desires and anticipations: things beyond the ordinary. In Sunday school, we sang about "Ivory Palaces" and "Whispering Hope." I had no idea what those exotic images were about. As a young adult, new awareness, new images, new expectations defined hope. It took on various meanings in the world, in my own value system. An exploration of hope brings to mind words from hymns. Each suggests different attributes of hope – its place in belief, its value in experience.

1. "Jesus, the Very Thought of Thee" (12th century) by Bernard of Clairvaux, a Cistercian monk. This is highly introspective and idealized: hope enriches the life experience but looks to life beyond death.

> *Jesus, the very thought of Thee with sweetness fills my breast;*
> *but sweeter far Thy love to see, and in Thy presence rest.*

> *O Hope of every contrite heart, O joy of all the meek,*
> *to those who fall, how kind Thou art! How good to those who seek!*

> *But what to those who find, Ah, this nor tongue nor pen can show:*
> *The love of Jesus, what it is none but His loved ones know.*

> *Jesus, our only Joy be Thou, as Thou our Prize wilt be;*
> *Jesus, be Thou our Glory now, and through eternity.*

2. "I Greet Thee, Who My Sure Redeemer Art" (1545) by John Calvin, the Swiss reformer. It relates Christ's identity to life experience. (It reflects the idea of individualism rising from the Renaissance.) It is specific; it is personal.

> *I greet Thee, who my sure Redeemer art,*
> *my only Trust and Savior of my heart,*
> *who pain didst undergo for my poor sake;*
> *I pray Thee from our hearts all cares to take.*

> *Thou are the life, by which alone we live,*
> *and all our substance and our strength receive;*
> *sustain us by Thy faith and by Thy power,*
> *and give us strength in every trying hour.*

Our hope is in no other save in Thee;
our faith is built upon Thy promise free;
Lord, give us peace, and make us calm and sure,
that in Thy strength we evermore endure.

3. "Guide Me, O Thou Great Jehovah", (1745) by William Williams, a Welsh evangelical. In this hymn, hope is implicit, but its value relates to realities in this life's experiences – a call for God's involvement in life's hardships. (These are hard times for Welsh coal-mining families in pre-Industrial Revolution Europe.)

Guide me, O Thou great Jehovah, pilgrim through this barren land;
I am weak, but Thou art mighty: lead me with Thy powerful hand;
bread of heaven, bread of heaven, feed me till I want no more.

When I tread the verge of Jordan, bid my anxious fears subside;
death of death, and hell's destruction, land me safe on Canaan's side;
songs of praises, songs of praises, I will ever give to Thee.

Each hymn considers hope a vital part of spiritual identity. Each implies a present-future connection.

Each hymn reflects a particular human environment. The writers attempt to express the impact (and mystery) of God-with-us, particularly as this affects personal identity and real life. Hope identifies this element of mystery. This calls to mind a Good Friday hymn, "O Sacred Head, Now Wounded":

What language can I borrow to thank Thee, dearest Friend,
for this Thy dying sorrow, Thy pity without end?
O make me Thine forever; and should I fainting be,
Lord, let me never, never outlive my love to Thee.

"What _language_ can I borrow" does not mean Greek or English. It is the grammar of experience (terms and ways to express meaningfully faith and experience). This tool (skill) equips us for spiritual experience: it helps us be comfortable with stimuli that address the spirit, mystery.

We need to consider a broader use of "grammar." Every language has a grammar to help use it clearly and well. It is sets of principles used to present and communicate information in a field of knowledge – some purely objective, some more interpersonal. (Each has its own premises, terms, definitions, symbols.) It is the bridge that enables persons to relate biographical experience with biological mechanisms, i.e., happenings live on as memories.

There is a grammar for mathematics: measurements and relationships of quantities (using numbers and symbols). Technical skills (computer programs) use a special grammar for electronic operations. On the playing field, we learn the grammar for both games and sportsmanship.

Our explorations deal with a more sublime part of our biographical reality: the grammar of faith experience, self, and spiritual experience. It is self in the world, with others. It is also creature and Creator - and a richer understanding of self as self. It is not engineered; it is not part of our genetic development. It is about faith's impact on what we consider real. The grammar of experience deals with options more than predictions. It engenders spiritual security in human experience. It is essential for covenant. The grammar of spiritual experience deals with "mystery" – what finds us more than what we find.

God initiated covenant face-to-face with Abraham (Gen 18:19):

> *I have chosen [Abraham] that he may charge his children and his household after him to keep the way of the Lord by doing righteousness and justice; so that the Lord may bring about... what he promises.*

Long after that covenant, long after the Exodus and wilderness wandering, the chosen people sought an identity. Neither Abraham's nor Moses' covenant encounters left them a workable model of a visible nation. Israel struggled to define its grammar of experience for God's initiatives, covenant. Israel looked around at neighboring cultures: they observed kings and armies and walls and weapons. Abraham's descendants chose kings, built armies, constructed citadels, pursued martial conflicts, collected loot (and were looted). More tangible, earth-oriented goals of might, wealth, and strategic wisdom took priority over *righteousness and justice*.

These goals shaped a new ethos, culture. Jeremiah contrasts might, wealth, and wisdom with neglected elements of covenant goals (Jer 9:23-24):

> *Thus says the Lord: 'Do not let the wise boast in their wisdom, do not let the mighty boast in their might, do not let the wealthy boast in their wealth; but let those who boast boast in this, that they understand and know me, that I am the Lord; I act with steadfast love, justice, and righteousness in the earth, for in these things I delight'*

Other prophets call for revival of covenant bonds, e.g., Zechariah's witness (Zech 4:6): *This is the word of the Lord ... 'Not by might or by power, but by my spirit.'* It is a stark reminder: God's chosen are covenant people (spiritually bonded); **and** covenant people have a calling: service, not conquest.

Our explorations of Faith and Love draw on Paul's refinements of the grammar of experience. The Holy Spirit comes to Saul. That divine initiative brought Saul's/Paul's response: a new creation *in Christ* (II Cor 5:17). It happens in this world's human experience. Biographical reality affects how one lives life. And testimony of this is revelation: a *human being* perceives of life in terms of birth and death, but not so the *spiritual being* (Rom 8:38-39):

> *For I am convinced that neither death, nor life, nor angels, nor*
> *rulers, nor things present, nor things to come, nor powers, nor*
> *height, nor depth, nor anything else in all creation, will be able*
> *to separate us from the love of God in Christ Jesus our Lord.*

The grammar of experience links with mystery: the "hope of glory" (Col 1:27).

We observe how Paul alters the grammar of experience. The Damascus Road event moved him "outside the box" of his Pharisaical confines. His multicultural heritage made it possible to entertain the new perspective. And still – 2,000 years later – the Church discovers elements of faith from diverse cultural traditions. Differing worldviews enrich a dynamic Christian faith.

Spiritual traditions perceive the dwelling place of their divinities as part of creation or away from it. The Greek gods dwelt atop Mount Olympus. Israel envisioned God "up" in space beyond the firmament. Christian tradition celebrates God-with-us in human form as Jesus, and then as Spirit following Pentecost ... we are not alone.

Some cultures perceive divine presence inherent in all creation. It is part of their grammar of experience. God does not "do" creation, then remain apart from it; rather, God abides – a covenant presence upholding rightness and integrity. This is affirmed in the opening of New Zealand's Maori version of the Lord's Prayer.

Our more familiar opening of the Lord's Prayer is: "*Our Father, who art **in** heaven.*" The Maori rendering is:

> "*Eternal Spirit,*
> *Earth-maker, Pain bearer, Life-giver,*

Source of all that is and that shall be,
Father and Mother of us all,
*Loving God, **in whom** is heaven.*"

Note the differences in the grammar of experience. Our more familiar version identifies heaven as a separate place where God abides. The Maori rendering speaks of heaven as the environment for those bonded in covenant fellowship.

Faith <u>now</u> melds with fulfillment <u>then</u>! In the interim (between <u>now</u> and <u>then)</u> Paul discerns an essential element in the grammar of experience: Faith is not a passive experience. Paul's Damascus Road encounter generates covenant exchange: we are *in Christ,* and consequently *Christ in us* is both a <u>now</u> and a <u>then</u> experience (hope). This covenant exchange is the energy that forms and energizes our *followership,* our initiatives as stewards.

Exploration III is about hope. Here we turn to Peter's experience. His face-to-face involvement with Jesus' ministry was extensive: three years travelling, teaching, healing, crucifixion, resurrection, ascension, Pentecost. Peter poignantly illustrates a struggle to find a grammar for spiritual experience.

After the resurrection, the Lord meets Peter at the Sea of Galilee (John 21). Jesus commissions Peter to a ministry: "feed" sheep/lambs. Jesus here ordains Peter. This eludes Peter until he experiences the full impact of the resurrection – hope, his "rock" as a spiritual being (I Peter 1:3):

Blessed be the God and Father of our Lord Jesus Christ!
By his great mercy he has given us a new birth into a living
hope through the resurrection of Jesus Christ from the dead.

That revelation wakens Peter's faith as a steward of life *in Christ,* not just an alumnus of Jesus' inner circle. The impact of the resurrection clarifies the grammar of spiritual experience; it underscores *"whole and lasting life"* Jesus promised prior to his death (John 14:18ff):

I will not leave you orphaned [desolate]. I'm coming back. In
just a little while the world will no longer see me, but you're
going to see me because I am alive and you're about to come
alive. At that moment you will know that I'm in the Father,
and you're in me, and I'm in you.

(Note about *"you're going to see me."* "To see," in the grammar of faith experience, means to know the presence and be made whole. The old covenant mechanism was different: to attain holiness by the law).

The common thread (in Peter's and Paul's encounters with Christ) is grace. Grace opens self to the value and beauty of God's initiatives, their benefits. This is the hope dimension in John 3:16. It is response, not attainment; it is personal, not private. Rebirth is soul-transforming, orienting self to new perspectives of service. A spiritual being retools with new values.

Transformation *in Christ* renews the inner self (Jer 31:31ff). Our behavior (action) is energized by covenant rightness. Mind, heart, and action no longer work randomly, impulsively; they correlate (Rom 8:28):

> *We know that all things work together for good for those who*
> *love God, for those who are called according to his purpose.*

(Note: Recall Jesus' use of good in Matt 7:17: *"… every good tree bears good fruit. …"* The Greek word translated *good* for the tree indicates a <u>quality</u> of the tree itself. The word *good* for the fruit indicates its <u>benefit</u> for the user.) The steward bears good (holiness) that benefits others. Stewardship:

- What it is: furthering God's good and right in this human
    experience.
- How it works: initiatives in relationships (groups, commu-
    nities, personal).
- Why it is important: it offers life a dimension that biology
    cannot.

A steward's life is exploration into God. Faith brings a new inner order. (The disciplines of medicine, psychiatry, and sociology all affirm such integration is important for health.)

A senior steward welcomes new capacity for grace: readiness for what makes whole. Faith and love clarify choices: good habits, bad habits; helpful attitudes, hurtful attitudes; open minds, closed minds; lovable qualities, unlovable qualities; grace-full, grace-less. Christian hope conditions present motivations and expectations for continuity. John Newton says in "Amazing Grace," verse 4:

The Lord has promised good to me, His word my <u>hope</u> assures;
He will my shield and portion be as long as life endures.

Hope is the fruit of resurrection confidence and expectation. Confidence is its reality; expectation is life's continuity beyond time. Hope resolves uncertainties; it makes the partial whole (I Cor 13:8a,10). Hope frees us from a need to speculate about what is yet-to-come. Christian hope is neither escapism nor fantasy; it is both present awareness and promised outcome.

In modern life, it is a challenge to keep this kind of hope. Henry Emerson Fosdick notes this in "God of Grace and God of Glory," *verse 3:*

Cure Thy children's warring madness, bend our pride to Thy control;
Shame our wanton, selfish gladness, rich in things and poor in soul.
Grant us wisdom, grant us courage, lest we miss Thy Kingdom's goal.

Christian hope is an action term (verb). It creates no earthly Utopia or fixes on a secular ideal. An apt New Testament usage connects hope with *parousia*, the Greek word for the end of earth-time, when life beyond death is fully in God's glory. But it is glory beginning now with our response to the Lord's initiatives. That's glory in life and glory beyond death. (I Peter 1:13, Peterson):

So roll up your sleeves, put your mind in gear, be totally ready
to receive the gift that's coming when Jesus arrives.

Hope – along with Faith and Love – is an inherent part of life *in Christ.* New birth engenders new spiritual DNA. Life is affected not just by our biological genetic programming, but by the measure of God's nature. The grammar of spiritual experience confirms our identity as stewards.

Matthew 25:21 (Peterson) commends those *in Christ*: "*Good work! You did your job well. From now on be my partner.*"

In v34, Jesus confirms the stewards' hope: "*...you are blessed by my Father! Take what's coming to you...It's been ready for you since the world's foundation.*"

We explore qualities of hope in the following **Meditations.**

Meditation Thirty

Some seniors give a nod to "after-life," or just "wait" for death.
Christian seniors expect life beyond death.
The readiness is redemptive, healing.
It need not be a morbid exercise.
We assess faith seriously. We let God's initiatives thrive in us.
We review how fully we let love affect us –
and we review the quality of love we share.
This exercise may surprise us with a fresh readiness for glory!
That's the power of hope, so strong we are its prisoners.
If our assessment makes us feel insecure, repent; repentance
strengthens the spirit's pulse for new exploration.
Eugene Peterson's translation of Psalm 51:10ff expresses this forcefully:
*God, make a fresh start in me, shape a Genesis week from the
chaos of my life. Don't throw me out with the trash
or fail to breathe holiness in me.
Bring me back from gray exile, put a fresh wind in my sails!*

Don't Fence Me In – or Out

*God created humankind in his image, in the image of God he created them. God
blessed them.* (Gen 1:27, Peterson)
*You won't die! God knows the moment you eat from the tree, you'll see what's
going on. You'll be just like God, knowing everything ranging all the way from
good to evil.* (Gen 3:3-4, Peterson)
*My grace is enough; it's all you need. My strength comes into its own in your
weakness.* (II Cor 12:9, Peterson)
*God, our God, will take care of the hidden things, but the revealed things are
our business. It is up to us to attend to what is revealed.* (Deut 29:29, Peterson)

Cole Porter's 1934 song expresses a goal of persons pioneering in the great unsettled stretches of land west of the Mississippi River:

Give me land, lots of land, under starry skies above –
Don't fence me in!
Let me ride through the wide open country that I love –
Don't fence me in!
Let me be by myself in the evenin' breeze,
and listen to the murmur of the cottonwood trees –
Don't fence me in!

When life issues constrain us, the metaphor of *wide open spaces* revives hope in our more free inner spirits.

Consider the old saw "Life begins at 40." Retirement is not close, but we think of days less fettered to schedules and imposed circumstances. We daydream about unfulfilled aspirations, stolen opportunities, and lost choices. Assuring our well-being persists as a concern; diminishing supports are an issue. We strive to save and safeguard resources for contingencies.

We cherish "walls" that protect selfhood … without causing too much isolation. Robert Frost articulates this irony in his poem "Mending Walls," which we noted earlier. On the one hand, barriers mean separation:
Something there is that doesn't love a wall....
However, it is good to respect personal boundaries:
Good fences make good neighbors.
The Genesis creation narrative addresses this. Eden is often idealized as perfected open space. Eden is holiness in all its glory. It is there for humans to access and use freely … except for the tree in a small separated area.

The tempter notes the tree's bounty. Eve says it is *korban* (Hebrew, meaning set apart, fenced off, a God space). The tempter infers *korban* may not mean "forbidden," perhaps just suggests "caution."

The tempter introduces one of history's perennial themes: "*Something there is that doesn't love a wall* [separation, limit of control]." (Modern culture considers "free access" an imperative right; society expects total transparency, level playing fields.) The tempter implies: If God endows humans with this special trait (the Creator's image), should anything natural in this environment be fenced out?

With covenant comes mystery – "otherness," an uncomfortable quality in our earth-context. However, God's domain circumscribes natural law. It is in new covenant we share mystery by water and Word as life *in Christ*.

Consider Jacob: born to a family of promise that is itself part of a tribal culture. Jacob's life-journey is complex: an uncle's duplicity, two wives, 12 sons by four mothers, separation from in-laws, and eventually a reunion in the "fences" of home. He ventures beyond his home-fences. There he has a vision experience: a ladder with angels ascending and descending. He wakens, assured of God's blessing.

His spirit-journey includes another unreal encounter. Not a vision, but engagement with God – not on Jacob's home turf, but in God's unwalled creation space. It is a sacramental encounter. Jacob emerges with a reminder (a mark) – his persistent limp. Jacob becomes Israel – the steward of patriarchal promise. We observe new behaviors. His spiritual communion with God brings a covenant perspective – a changed outlook.

The family's saga moves to Egypt – enslavement and deliverance – the Exodus. The people (Israel) receive covenant "fences/walls" (Law) to define and promote holiness and rightness. The Law is a guide for faithfulness … often ignored.

Centuries later, Saul of Tarsus forcefully protects the sanctity of that covenant Law. He attacks Jesus' followers who claim allegiance to a *new* covenant sealed by the resurrection of the crucified Christ – Savior, Lord. Followers claim this covenant loyalty refines the "fence" of ancestral Law.

Saul goes to Damascus; *en route,* he encounters the risen Christ (an echo of Jacob's story). Away from walled Jerusalem's holy Temple and Ark, in wide-open spaces, Christ's holiness engulfs Saul. Saul becomes a new creation, marked with a new identity, a new name: Paul. It is mystic, sweet communion, a sacramental moment. Paul's experience is not uniquely private; it's an encounter experienced by others – although usually less startling. It recurs beyond Jerusalem, into the East, into Europe and beyond.

The Lord instituted a new global mission: "Love beyond borders." It's a communion and an earthly mission sanctioned with beyond-earthly mystery. Paul talks about it: *The mystery is this: Christ in you … you can look forward to sharing in God's glory. It's that simple.* (Col 1:28, Peterson)

Like Jacob, Paul carries an annoying physical uneasiness as a memory of that encounter. He asks God to remove whatever it is. God's response: *"My grace is enough."*

Life's stroll is seldom in a safely "fenced," landscaped garden. It's always a pioneering venture – weaving through and over and around earth-ordered events, relationships, choices, obstacles, neighbors' walls.

The soul thrives on Spirit-breath; God's grace sustains our human experience. Followers unfence their spirits and open the inner life-terrain to Christ. His energy is love; it steadies unsure beginnings with nail-scarred hands.

Seniors age. Life's growing pains revisit us – more like second adolescence (growing older) than second childhood (growing up). Our physical needs drain energy; pastoral inputs bring tranquillity. We feel more and more bound by natural conditions; perhaps it's time to deal with unresolved spiritual challenges.

Hope is a vital nutrient for seniors. (Not fate/karma – that vaguely assumes life's choices are preordained.) Hope is spirit energy. It readies a spiritual being for mystery – waiting, prepared.

Israel passed through the Red Sea and began its wilderness journey. Wilderness seemed endless space, where God's promise withered in the arid environment. (That space/time seemed necessary for Israel to be ready to trust a Father's promises, different from Mother Nature's. Israel didn't realize affairs must be soul-size in order to prosper in the land of promise, **and** the promised glory ... but Moses continued to trust in God.)

After 40 years, Moses looks toward the Promised Land looming across the Jordan River and says: "*God, our God, will take care of the hidden things, but the revealed things are our business. It is up to us to attend to what is revealed.*" (Deut 29:29)

A senior blessing I experience is readiness to draw on benefits from my own sacramental encounters. God and me, the holy neither fenced "in" nor "out." After four score years, I know what it is to be a steward of grace: it is sufficient, and *"grace will see me home."* I'm not home yet, so I still explore.

Exploration *in Christ* opens new options for fulfillment. Like skill for piano playing, I must practice the scales of my faith – I must do daily the exercises of love. God composes the music (the opus, the work) of my life story. My stewardship is: Hear the music in my soul and perform its pieces (jobs) with those I encounter. All these years I've done it in snatches. Ahead is the concluding coming together of my life story – an end-beginning of glory, the wonder of eternity.

This stirs an even more alluring serenity than Cole Porter's *"murmur of the evening breeze in the cottonwood trees."* Now it's *"the voice I hear falling on my ear"* – God's own voice, invitation: *"Let's commune and continue! Let my indwelling presence affect who you are and what you do."*

So I say *"Amen."* I accept the surprising power of grace – the eternal arch, a bridge by which the spiritual connects with and affects the natural. A senior self without fences who knows the greatness of God's faithfulness:

> *Pardon for sin and a peace that endureth,*
> *God's own dear presence to cheer and to guide;*
> *Strength for today and bright hope for tomorrow -*
> *Blessing all ours, with ten thousand beside!*

Paul observes: those baptized in Christ Jesus live in newness of life.
This new life is neither free-wheeling, nor immunized from sin.
It's life as cluttered as Simon Peter's (Peter's natural boldness
repeatedly clutters his followership).
Peter strives to r-e-a-c-h Jesus in the darkness of a stormy night when he
steps confidently out of a
fishing boat expecting to be supported over the water.
Suddenly Peter meets the other side of boldness – doubt.
Sinking he cries for deliverance.
"Newness of life" is seldom full-blown; it needs time to mature, to
generate spiritual courage, to become a "rock" – securing hope.
Spiritual maturity nears when God's r-e-a-c-h gets to your soul.
Hope, God's everlasting arms, r-e-a-c-h you with not-yet-visible security!

What's 'New' in Newness of Life?

But now faith in Jesus Christ makes clear the righteousness of God: His gift of grace justifies us through the redemption that is in Christ Jesus....Therefore we have peace with God. (Romans 3:21a, 22a, 24a; 5:1b)
What then are we to say? Should we continue in sin so grace may abound? By no means! (Romans 6:1-2a)
Those baptized in Christ Jesus live in newness of life. (Romans 6:3b,5c)
What then should we say – that the law is sin? By no means! (Romans 7:7a)
Now there is no condemnation for those who are in Christ Jesus. We are free to behave according to the law of the Spirit in Christ Jesus; we do not live by the law of sin and death. (Romans 8:1-2)

For 50 years in the pastorate, I began baptisms with these words: "Dearly beloved, baptism is an outward and visible sign of an inward and spiritual grace." When I heard these words as a child, I wondered what in baptism is "inward" and "outward."

At 12 years I was confirmed and received a first communion. I was anxious, wondering: Does confirmation put me especially near to God? How do I know? (Even a 12-year-old is aware of personal **un**rightness that quickens inner self-doubts and spiritual uncertainly.)

The more apt perspective in such moments is not what you think about God, but what God thinks about you.

Everyone's spiritual journey brings questions about spiritual inter-actions: what God does, what I do. Early in Christian experience, I learn God is trustworthy. And, early in life I know my own inconsistencies. If God is really God, I ask, can he honestly tolerate my inconsistency – in faith and action?

God works purposefully, not erratically. The prophets and psalms often stress this: *I made you, I created you with intention. I spoke, you were. My providence and generosity never cease … that is my grace!*

We praise the Creator's work with litanies of our Father's world with its birds, trees, flowers and waterfalls. There is order in creation: a natural law with patterns. The Bible goes further and brings us creatures in a covenant connection. The Bible indicates love and grace affect our natural patterns:

- Israel's saga: atonement restores one to the Law's rightness.
- A baptismal experience: new birth, new life, direction in the Spirit.

Still anxieties buffet us.

The thread of this anxiety: What does God see in any one of us? An answer is outside the framework of our cultural conditions. The answer rests in covenant bonding/fellowship (or lack of it!). A fellowship relationship is inherent in the *raison d'etre* of Creation.

God gives us a life of His devising. This life is able to resist – not his might (that never really comes under consideration) – but His love. Then, unexpectedly, we come face-to-face with the Cross – God re-creates!

Most of us are adept at pulling inside ourselves. It happens subtly, insidiously. It starts when we lose our innocence. This is more than moral simplicity. We lose our innocence when we use self as the source of 1) our standards, and 2) our social or spiritual behaviors. The enslavement begins when first we doubt others' love. We resolve that by asking: "How can I make others love me?"

We react defensively more than responsively. We contrive, even manipulate, responses. Emotional crutches support a maimed sense of personal value and worth. We examine behaviors and lost virtues to see what to redecorate, touch up, or even disguise! A gnawing unrest, like realizing we devalue an antique by tampering with an original finish.

Paul assures the restless Romans: *We have peace with God*. God loves us, redeems us, awaits our trust. Paul exhorts Christians to <u>own</u> their faith:
- grace assures rightness with God: we are created, re-created;
- faith (trust) thrives on the gift of God's indwelling Spirit;
- we work out our own right living to let the Holy Spirit shape hope.

God is with us in the Law: it marks pathways/lanes for living rightly, safely; signs indicate hazards. God is with us in the Holy Spirit: new inner direction for life's journey. Recall the Samaritan woman's new perception of *living* water (John 4). Capture the prodigal's release from tension when he heard the father's dramatic blessing: *Welcome home child* [not prodigal person!].

An elderly lady always went to the same post office branch – she liked the friendly clerks. In December, she waited in a long line. Someone mentioned she could get stamps from the lobby machine and save time. Appreciatively she replied: *"I know, but the machine won't ask me about my arthritis."*

Paul notes this gift of new life is communion + accountability. Our redeemed initiatives make new life real and visible. His rhetorical question: *What then are we to say? Should we continue in the same old patterns so God can continue to demonstrate grace? By no means.* (Romans 6:1)

We have peace with God. We are loved. We are a fellowship of the re-created – not sequestered, but scattered among friends and strangers. We are Spirit-borne stewards of God's expectations!

The Invitation to share at the Lord's Table includes the phrase: *"… and intend to lead a new life following the commandments."* Each experience is a recurring covenant commitment.

In this covenant we continue to honor the Law, the commandments. Now, we discover what we may have missed before our baptismal re-creation!
- *I the Lord am your God who brought you out of the land of Egypt.* Be stewards of redemption – don't let it go for nothing.
- *Have no other gods beside me.* Do not create/do things that supersede your spiritual bonding with God.

193

- *Do not swear falsely by the name of the Lord your God.* Use God's name and attributes rightly ... based on who/what God is/does.
- *Observe the Sabbath and keep it holy.* Set apart time and space in which the priority is closeness with God; find time and space to celebrate God's purposes as well as meet your own deadlines.

The communion Invitation begins: ... *intend to lead a new life.* Communion means: synchronize our behavior with God's will. This requires soul-searching choices: Am I impelled to follow my dreams blindly, or in communion do I find a fit between God's right and mine?

Two fathers were chatting about commitments and satisfactions:
#1 – *Let's play golf on Saturday.*
#2 – *I'm sorry, I can't. I'm taking my 11-year-old to a ballgame.*
#1 – *I didn't know you like baseball that much.*
#2 – *I don't, but I like my child that much!*

Seniors cherish spiritual moments – these keep real God's gifts of re-creation and sustaining grace. In faith we commit to works that are outward and visible signs of inner, spiritual grace.

Life's inner journey is seldom totally settled; change and conditions alter priorities. There is always a frontier to enter, to make habitable: a new residence, new address, new neighbors, new work environment, new rules, new expectations. Some frontiers are expansive and open; some are more restrictive and limiting.

Every frontier is a time/space for us to find new comfort by the Holy Spirit. It's sparked when God's right embeds itself more fully in us. So inspired, we find other like-spirited persons sharing this. In fellowship we find blessing even in quixotic conditions.

God loves you and me. The Lord relies on us to replicate His kind of love. The world suggests we assess our bounty as half-full or half-empty. Set that measure aside. You and your new life revel in a new dynamic. Gaze on and *r-e-a-c-h* to the Lord's sufficiency – never hope-empty, always hope-full!

Aging can be daunting – even discouraging – in spite of careful planning.
Where once we had courage enough (and to spare!),
now stark, debilitating realities overwhelm.
Those who refine and deepen faith and love are never barred from grace by
unexpected challenges and contingencies.
Spiritual beings season expectations with holy hope.
Faith is an ever-burning pilot flame igniting eternity's light even when
buffeted by ill winds in earth-life time.
The daily exercise of sharing love is grace continuing to ripen.
Covenant faith and love have qualities beyond earth time and space.
Hope anchors them and beckons our allegiance.
In the sweep of forever, this moment is both "already" and "not yet"!

More Than Your Wildest Dreams

God can do anything, you know – far more than you could ever imagine or guess or request in your wildest dreams! He does it not by pushing us around but by working his Spirit deeply and gently with us ... take in the extravagant dimensions of Christ's love. Reach out and experience the breadth! Test its length! Plumb the depths! Rise to the heights! Live full lives, full in the fullness of God.
(Ephesians 3:20, 18-19, Peterson)

I was in third grade; it was during World War II. Among my childlike whimsies I thought I had composed a well-known song! (My measure of ownership: I knew the melody and some words.) Its first line: "From the halls of Montezuma to the shores of Tripoli." A kind adult gently negotiated the burst of my creative bubble, and I continued skipping to the song I hadn't written!

Another cherished and spirit-uplifting bubble of hope: a summer holiday anticipating Miss Kingston's fourth-grade class. September came, and I was there. Two weeks later my father's bishop popped that bubble: he appointed my father to another church. We moved 10 days later.

I entered a new school, negotiated strange corridors, tried to pair unfamiliar names and faces in Mrs. Darling's fourth grade. I was an outsider – a new kid from some unheard-of town.

I was "inserted" in a group of children and their staked-out territory. I searched 26 sets of staring eyes; those same 26 sets of probing eyes scrutinized me, an intruder. It was their world; I trespassed its boundary. I was a no one amid someones. My hope for a happy school year was on shaky ground. My confidence bubble burst!

These experiences are a natural part of growing up (physically) and maturing (mentally, socially). Childhood's bubbles pop; adolescents' dreams fade; practicalities tangle adults' expectations. Aging often presses us to settle for diminished realties and truth. Adults devise systems of comfort and security, then we're shocked to discover "batteries" to energize those mechanisms weaken quickly. Bubbles keep bursting!

Spiritual life encounters this! Changing conditions pull the rug out from under us. Life crises outdistance our list of Bible-verse-solutions-for-every-situation. J.B. Phillips' insight rings true: "Your God is too small!"

Paul, in prison, writes to Christians in Asia Minor. He tells them God includes them in something magnificent. He challenges them to own a faith that carries beyond their *wildest dreams* (and crises)!

Ancient religions often had pantheons of specialized deities. Each deity related to specific needs. A sailor caught in a raging gale sought deliverance by the god of seas. Divine patronage addressed a need of the moment. Unlike Ali Baba's genie that offered wish-bundles, these gods targeted aid to devotees' specific issues: victory, health, family, money, harvest, offspring, vanity. Religious talk was about products/results sought from the gods.

Paul's evangelistic message swept through the Roman Empire like a mighty wind. It burst spiritual wish-bubbles and a focus on single-concern gods. Paul's God embraces human life in all its fullness and complexity. God partners with covenant cadres. Paul's God is not Lord of a particular devotee, culture, or nation. (A heretical turn from Israel's tradition!)

God re-creates and gathers a new human family: the church. Religious interaction takes a different direction: no longer "how to get God's attention," but how God-with-us affects our identity and then our service.

Paul's God empowers a body (the church, a collective of parts) for God's service. Local groups take up the calling. All witness to a now-and-forever experience: new life *in Christ*. This God-with-humans connection, this hope is more than people's *wildest dreams*!

Wherever persons share life *in Christ* there is judgment – a future outside present reality, a bodyless tomb, an end as beginning. The judgment requires a response ... even "no response" is a response!

Seniors confront the reality of death with a critical factor: an encounter with resurrection. Death is neither a last frontier, nor nothingness. We have life beyond death with God. This is the Easter reality.

Peter's experience takes him past his *wildest dreams*. He is an extraordinary example – this marshland of a life, this larger-than-life bumbler seeking a spiritual center of gravity. Christ labels him the church's rock of hope – *"and the gates of Hell shall not prevail!"* The church is God's people loose in the world, leavening the world, deflating illusory bubbles. It exposes false facades and illusory idolatries – all pretense of lasting hurt or evil. The assault is against whatever tries to afflict rightness with pernicious anemia!

But remember: God attends to particulars, each signaling the start of something bigger. Each fragment of renewal is evidence of God himself, not a proof about religion. An ailment healed, an addled mind calmed, darkness unblinded, lameness mobilized, dysfunctional relationships remolded for joy! This is how God's domain grows.

God's every intention calls for human action. The New Testament gathers such actions under the canopy verb to love. Paul speaks of this in the text: *Experience the breadth! Test the length! Plumb the depths! Rise to the heights! Live in God's fullness!*

We explore initiatives that become foundations for faith. Discover the extravagant dimensions of God's love. Love is not a hobby fashioned to personal tastes. Love is an unwieldy treasure of verbs that give life hope! God is ready to be involved with hopes we are ready to discard! Langston Hughes' short verse *"A Dream Deferred"* poses a question:

What happens to a dream deferred?
Does it dry up
Like a raisin in the sun?
Or fester like a sore –
And then run?
Does it stink like rotten meat?
Or crust and sugar over –
Like a syrupy sweet?
Maybe it just sags
Like a heavy load.
Or does it explode?

What happens to stewardship opportunities you defer? Do you just watch them dry up, like a raisin in the sun, and eventually die?

Not so with God's promises – those untamed, free-range ones you consider *wildest dreams*! Redemption happens when the Spirit finds faith that initiates loving action. God guides, God provides.

Seniors cherish special memories, joyous recollections, fulfilments preserved through time. During spiritual meditation and reflection, gather these beautiful thoughts as a banquet for the soul. That is fine. And, when reality seems bent on bursting your "bubbles," draw near to God and be nourished. That is good for your soul – it revives your love verb-power!

Perhaps your hope seems a bubble in reality. How glibly people say: *"I hope it doesn't rain,"* or *"I hope the plane is on time."* Such hope is without substance – lost in *if, might, could, maybe* … and technical glitches. In such instances, hope's foundation is a collection of possibilities.

Everyone *in Christ* includes faith and love in earth-life experience. These virtues define self and behaviors (our identity) that the church (our community) expresses outwardly.

Hope's substance dwells in life beyond death. Till then, it is a destination soaring beyond creation's *tohu-wa-bohu*, beyond the edges of earth's time and space. It is the habitat of what is real and everlasting life. Seniors prepare for this transition.

Hope becomes an event when a believer reaches earth-life's end. It's the end that is always a beginning.

Aging often brings a flood of the unexpected.
We downsize from a home where marriage and family "happened."
We retire from involvements that pursued worthy objectives.
Social activities seem repetitive, a bit tiring.
Without warning our untested hope dims.
Senior's spiritual exploration leads to a truer, more enticing hope.
Fresh hope sets a new perspective.
Mature hope gives a clearer vision of blessing and expectation.
Hope's horizon previews more promise, less mystery.
The time is right to freshen up hope!

The Familiar Is Gone Away –
but Behold What's Waiting

Jerusalem, stand up! Shine! Your new day is dawning. The glory of the Lord shines brightly on you...Israel, open your eyes! Look around! Crowds come. Your off-spring are on their way from distant lands...I, the holy Lord God of Israel, do this to honor your people, so they will honor me. (Is 60:1,3,4,9c)
I saw a new heaven and a new earth. The first had disappeared...Then I saw new Jerusalem, that holy city, coming down from God like a bride ready to join her espoused...A voice: "I am making everything new." (Rev 21:1,2b,4b,5)

Each stage of growth brings new kinds of questions: 1) As children: *"What is your name?"* – <u>identity</u> 2) With new work colleagues or college classmates: *"Where are you from?"* – <u>community</u>. 3) With work team partners: *"What skills do you bring so our work goals are more effective?"* – <u>continuity</u>.

Everyone seeks <u>identity</u> – a place in space.

Everyone wants connections - <u>community</u>.

In Thornton Wilder's *Our Town*, Rebecca Gibbs talks with her brother George. She mentions the letter her friend Jane received from their pastor. The envelope read: "Jane Crofut, Crofut Farm, Grover's Corners, Sutton County, New Hampshire, USA, North America, Western Hemisphere, the Earth, the Solar System, the Universe, the Mind of God." (Rebecca adds this comment: *"and the postman brought it all the same!"*)

Everyone yearns for <u>continuity</u>.

TV talk shows interview people saddened by unresolved crises and loss: a missing loved one, some injustice, a life-changing accident. Each indicates yesterday's expectations now vanished.

Remember a childhood delight at the seashore – building sandcastles? Suddenly, a wave sweeps away fruits of enthusiastic labor. The child is saddened; good things shouldn't go away so unexpectedly.

A gentleman came to my Pastor's Office in New Delhi. He was moving elsewhere and asked if we might take his dog. Residents in our neighborhood were Hindi-speaking; he knew we were English-speaking. His dog only understood commands in English. He wanted the loved pet to face minimal stress in the change of home. His concern: community and continuity.

I received a letter in New Delhi, mailed seven days earlier from a rural post office in Iowa. It brought greetings and prayer support from a Sunday school sixth-grader. The envelope had only four words: "Rev Smith Church India." In a world of seven billion, how did that letter ever connect so correctly, so directly?

Israel – the chosen people – face one identity crisis after another. Through all uncertainty, Jerusalem symbolized hope – an idealized milk-and-honey oasis on a hill. Even exiled in Babylon, Isaiah recalled this image of Jerusalem to inspire weeping Israel.

The vision of Jerusalem: God's people together, safe and secure in a just social order. Israel's never-settled history sees the dream set in a more distant time, more vague space.

Revelation sets Jerusalem in another time/space frame – a new age! The first heaven, the first Earth, the sea – gone! (The Greek word translated "gone" indicates something totally nonexistent – a kind of evaporation from time, without identity in what we consider space.) Our familiar – vanishes. Then what?

"I'm making everything new!" Not updating, redecorating, changing worn out parts of an old covenant – but a radically new creation. Revelation's *everything new* is new kind: not previously present, and of a higher excellence. Wow! (Did we miss something God did between *Isaiah* and *Revelation*?

Perhaps. Did we miss Paul's mysterious twinkling-of-an-eye moment that reframes history? Perhaps.

Mysterious ways are often not recognized because they seem dressed in ordinary trappings! Like the starting point of "life beyond death" begins with, well, death!

Consider King Herod's call for Judah's census. Herod's local decree was part of Rome's empirewide call. Rome wanted an updated, universal tax base. It set in motion radical implications – involving both Jewish religion and Roman politics. It initiated personal changes for many. Scripture links them. They can be noted as matters of fact, or, matters of faith – or both!

God calls Mary – to bear His holiness. God calls Joseph – to trust faith affects reality. God calls simple shepherds – to accept and share good news. A new star calls the learned – to pursue new perspectives of spiritual and mental creativity. Calls set transitions in motion; they coincide in a unique human encounter: Emmanuel – God-with-us!

These calls shift priorities and focus: from Jerusalem to Jesus, from city to child, from citadel to savior, from sacred history to sacred mystery. The old song: *"Jerusalem the golden with milk and honey blessed"*; the new song: *"O little town of Bethlehem … the hopes and fears of all the years are met in thee tonight."* The shift: from Israel at ease and protected in God's anticipated royal domain, to a here-and-now steward responsibility for God's mission work plan.

Such calls affect us with a new identity: God equips us to be bearers of grace! *"Joy of heaven to earth come down; fix in us thy humble dwelling."* Paul says this *"reconciles"* – marks us as "found," i.e., we regain our competence and confidence as God's image. Paul continues: *"The mystery in a nutshell is this: Christ is in you."* (Col. 1:27)

Our missionary appointment: Centenary Methodist Church, New Delhi. A new building, set on what was then the frontier of burgeoning expansion of a capital city. The new structure honored 100 years of the Methodist mission in India. Centenary's ministry pioneered a second century of stewardship calling.

Beyond our compound was an expanse of construction. New residential colonies to house experienced personnel called in from regional assignments – essential staff for the new government's offices and services. Thousands of families, tens of thousands of individuals of all ages, were uprooted from familiar comforts: homes, first languages, extended families, schools, spiritual fellowships. Routine daily securities (identity, community) disappeared; many new challenges (discontinuity) required urgent resolution.

Our assignment: develop an English-speaking congregation. (English was the "link" for India's more-than-20 major regional languages.) On our first Sunday, fewer than 25 were present; even fewer seemed "at home." People were polite, but not relaxed. It was more like a waiting room than a spiritual family gathering. My primary pastoral function for the coming months was clear: listen!

Worshippers came from varying denominational traditions – only one lifelong Methodist family. Few had experience in congregational leadership. The bishop agreed it was wise to minimize usual institutional formalities. Ministry centered on spiritual enrichment and bonding; growth was vigorous.

As our congregation demonstrated more unity and community, its officials wanted to assess our direction. In a serene, natural setting some 8,000 feet in the Himalayan foothills, officials (and their families) spent four days defining characteristics essential for our common life. We assessed resources and expectations. The outcome – our calling, not our programs.

We now identified ourselves differently: Centenary was in us, more than we were in Centenary. Christ bonded us to Him, to each other, to mission and service as the body called Centenary! There was no impulse to transfer fond memories from "home" settings to New Delhi. We were engaged in an Emmaus walk, not a New Jerusalem reverie.

Our diverse backgrounds enriched the quality of caring and service. We took personal and collective ownership of a resource: love. A primary motivation: be spendthrifts of God's love. We especially served the neglected, unsettled and disenfranchised around us. In later years, members reflected, we bonded as a fellowship more than united with a church. We knew the mystery Charles Wesley expresses: *"Love divine, all love's excelling ... fix in us thy humble dwelling ..."*

It is very human to feel lost when removed from the familiar. The Lord's call: serve Him, and in doing this, discovering His will becomes a "happening." Perhaps the mystery of God-with-us is more fully evident when we read the phrases from *Our Town* in reverse order. Begin with "The mind (or heart) of God" back to "Crofut Farm, Jane Crofut" (<u>or</u>, your own address, then your name)! That traces your identity – connection (community) – continuity! It is a giant step of faith to trust someone when your world becomes a topsy-turvy Something Else.

Hope is faith's anchor. Hope in life beyond death adds the aura of glory to faith. Life beyond death surely moves us beyond what is earth-treasure. Hope's contribution is the quality of completeness, satisfying grace.

Rabindranath Tagore, the Nobel Prize-winning Indian poet, expresses this mystery in his poem-prayer *Crossing (XVIII)*:

I know that this life, missing its ripeness in love, is not altogether lost.
I know that the flowers that fade in the dawn, the streams that stray in the desert, are not altogether lost.
I know that whatever lags behind in this life laden with burden is not altogether lost.
I know that my dreams still unfulfilled, and my melodies still unstruck, are clinging to some lute-strings of Yours, and they are not altogether lost.

Meditation Thirty-Four

The sacrament of Holy Communion celebrates life in Christ.
It is not simply a corrective mechanism like a pilot uses
when an aircraft strays from assigned flight patterns.
Our senior exploration celebrates both grace experienced
and grace anticipated. It nurtures covenant rightness in life.
In maturity grace is less particular, more expansive, as assurance
of promise awaits.
The sacrament of Holy Communion celebrates life in Christ.
The Lord gathers his own to celebrate hope.
Thanksgiving binds with expectation: a holy life prepared for me,
wholeness, a life redeemed for eternal joy.
Bless the Lord, O my soul, and forget not all His benefits.

God's Purpose-Driven Invitation

Therefore, my beloved…work out your own salvation with fear and trembling; for it is God who is at work in you, enabling you both to will and to work for his good pleasure. (Phil 2:12b-13)

The church family gathers for the Lord's Supper; it is a community celebration. A local fellowship bonds in the Spirit. Symbolically it extends far beyond that grouping. Consider features of this thanksgiving (*Eucharist*):

- It is a new creation moment! Come as you are to connect purposefully with the source of blessing.
- The community gathering is personal, but not private. God values each self; God's valuing unifies the fellowship.
- Our presence honors the Host's initiative; none "earn" a place.
- Communion interaction affirms our commitment to be a right and faithful steward; it does not reflect achievements – individual or collective.
- This is a new creation moment. Come as you are!

The invitation is purposeful, not a casual religious curiosity.

Our text reflects Paul's grief – his response to news received about the church at Philippi. The fellowship suffers because members choose to privatize spirituality. It indicates an elitist segment setting its own measures of goodness and propriety. Paul raises the image of "belonging" – not a human choice but a God-established collective, integrated parts making a whole. The body accepts Christ's purpose-driven mission: to be leaven and salt for the new creation.

Paul captures afresh the excitement of a new creation first perceived by Jeremiah, Ezekiel. God hides a soul (person) in each handful of clay awaiting eternity's blessing. It is the seed-promise of *shalom*, holiness, wholeness, completeness, unfettered joy. God breathes this into every self at birth; faith gives it identity, the Spirit nurtures development in bonding at the Lord's Table.

In the fullness of time – when the time is right – the Savior comes and confirms this new creation. His resurrection seals its promise. The Lord of creation commissions this new community: let the Holy Spirit germinate unawakened seed so love's redeeming work bears fruit.

Paul strives to clarify this in terms of our human experience. We are saved by grace. We are justified by faith. We own the work of our salvation. At this Lord's Table, we celebrate our part in His purpose-driven community. Here we come to *work out our own salvation ... and work for God's good pleasure*. We do not separate from the Lord. We connect with glory.

Scripture presents reliable elements and safe parameters as together the body pursues this goal:

1) Each member is a self-in-community. Community indicates belonging, a fruit of shared faith. Here we learn the grammar of faith experience.

An elementary teacher guided her class as the students mastered the new grammar of computers. A boy reads words printed on the screen: "The computer wants to know your name." (The lad forgot that he "speaks" with his computer by keying in data, e.g., a password, or in this case, his name.) The teacher, at a nearby desk, heard the boy whisper to the screen: *My name is David.* Faith is the universal password for benefits of the Lord's Table.

2) We are God's covenant community. The covenant is more than rules of order. It is the continuum of God's presence ... life to life, age to age. This spiritual energy refreshes and impels the church's life and service.

In the biography/movie, *A River Runs Through It,* Norman MacLean traces his family's early 20th-century pioneering in Montana's Big Sky country. The family's dreams and identity mature in an environment shared with this river. The river is a catalyst – real and symbolic – which binds and strengthens the family. Without the river, Montana would just be a wilderness with individual lives surprised by a nonending series of arbitrary obstacles.

The *"river runs through it"* symbolizes cohesion and energy. This bonds the family and empowers members to redeem the hurts and wrongs of their world. It echoes the image in *Revelation*: the city of God, with a river running through it, and trees with leaves that heal (body and soul). A Christian covenant community draws from life's healing stream: a vital wellspring of worship, fellowship, giving, caring, service. This nourishes, matures, provides direction and ultimate purpose.

3) The body's essential characteristic is singleness of heart. Each member is competent to know evil as evil and not yield to its sway.

Our Invitation to the Lord's Table: *All that do truly and earnestly repent of your sins, and are in love and charity with your neighbors, and intend to lead a new life following the commands of God, and walk from henceforth in his holy ways, draw near with faith and take this holy sacrament to your comfort.* (Note: "comfort" here means "to empower, to urge forward" – recall the visual image noted earlier of a plowman using a prod urging oxen to move on.)

We do not come sinless, but to accept forgiveness. We offer readiness for God to renew, make a change. Christ's sacrificial holiness heals festering temptations; God's grace affects us. To receive that blessing—to give ourselves permission—affects everything else we do in life!

The Invitation is God's preemptive assurance of friendship. We come, commune, now ready to be one more hope God has for the world. It moves us into the mysterious confluence of mercy and grace.

The parable of the prodigal son includes the phrase: *But while the son was still far off.* Why that sentence, unless the Father went to the gate every evening at twilight hoping some wayfarer might indeed be his child. The Father waits not with a list of prenatal expectations and postnatal grievances. He waits with a robe and a ring and an embrace – assurance of belonging and empowerment, the child's welcome to a new life prepared.

The invitation carries a purpose-driven intention. A foretaste now; a fulfillment waiting to welcome the family member to life beyond death – hope made ready!

Hope Abides

We all live off [Jesus'] generous bounty,
gift after gift after gift.
We got the basics from Moses,
and then this exuberant giving and receiving,
This endless knowing and understanding –
all this came through Jesus, the Messiah.
No one has ever seen God,
not so much as a glimpse.
This one-of-a-kind God-Expression [Jesus],
who exists at the very heart of the Father,
has made him plain as day.

(John 1:16-18, Peterson)

In Greek mythology, Zeus gifts Pandora a box and tells her not to open it. She does. Out fly all evils that infest the world. The last thing to emerge is hope, a resource to counter the unpredictable effects of evil. This was an ancient explanation of how to cope with a fate-shaped life.

Our exploration secures us as spiritual beings. Faith is our response to God's re-creating initiatives. Jesus' acts of grace happened in his public ministry, passion, resurrection, ascension. These prepare us for a Pentecost experience – God-with-us as the Holy Spirit. Faith wakens God-intended love. Our practice of love generates hope. This is the gist of the doxology we find in John 1:16-18 (above).

Hope is the lifeline bridging human experience with life beyond death, the temporal and the eternal. It redeems present time. It does not define the future; rather it extends life's reach beyond "now." Faith that initiates love and love that initiates hope are the covenant's chain of holiness and wholeness … beyond our time and space. God's loving-kindness, mercy, grace, is the energy of continuity.

Hope is part of Jewish and Christian covenant traditions. Israel depicted creation in the grammar of an earthly reality they/we are part of. "Glory" was perceived as grandeur attained by power and wealth in a social order: kings and kingdoms, fortresses and armies. It was a "glory" deformed by the conflicting values copied from **un**chosen neighboring nations.

What is unright prods and impels leaders and prophets to anticipate God as re-creator, one with the at-the-beginning creator. It moved Abraham, it stirred the wilderness wandering, it eased the despair of the nation in captivity. Isaiah cites words of promise (43:14a,15,19a):

Thus says the Lord, your redeemer, the Holy One of Israel … 'I am the Lord, your Holy One, the Creator of Israel, your King … I am about to do a new thing.'

Years later, the end of the first century of the Christian era, John of Patmos wrote (Rev 21:1,3a,4, Peterson):

I saw heaven and earth re-created. Gone the first Heaven, gone the first earth, gone the sea … 'Look! Look! God has moved into the neighborhood, making his home with men and women! They're his people, he's their God. … Death is gone for good – tears gone, crying gone, pain gone – all the first order of things gone.'

Hope abides – then, still. This resonates with Paul's affirmation that change is part of our spiritual experience.

We age, we change old perceptions! My childhood images of a new heaven and earth imitated settings in film epics like *Ben Hur* and *Quo Vadis*. *Revelation*, especially physical details in chapter 21, became Hollywood gates of pearl, structures laden with precious jewels, streets of gold. The contending hoards and contending forces in Revelation 19 became the Roman army versus an army of Christian slaves.

Movie technology offers radically new options about this universe (often more of creation as warfare than holy beauty). Other solar systems and galaxies are scattered in light-years of space. Science seeks common elements in this universe – outer physical worlds and inner psychological ones.

It is important to acknowledge and explore the spiritual part of our inner creation! This sets no essential tension between faith and science. It prods us ("comforts" us) to explore the grammar of spiritual experience; a grammar that uses familiar terms to open our perceptions to unexpected options.

The risen Christ – a changed form of the pre-Crucifixion Jesus – passed from our presence, beyond earth's clouded atmosphere. In a short time, he returns in Spirit-form – a presence whose effects are palpable but not visible. The Lord spoke of this earlier at the end of John 13 and opening of 14 (Peterson):

> *I am with you only a little longer. ... Live by the rhythms of grace, don't be overwhelmed with anxiety. Trust covenant love. I go to be with the Father, and where my Father is are many resting places. I go to make them ready and will come again to bring us together in that new communion.*

Jesus speaks of covenant love; from that comes hope. Peter speaks of hope with his special pastoral perspective, his years of personal interaction with Jesus. Peter's hope is always a benefit, a blessing of life in Christ. Hope is the "fruit" of God's love. Peterson expresses Peter's insights this way (II Peter 1:3a,5-9a):

> *Everything that goes into a life of pleasing God has been miraculously given to us. ... So don't lose a minute in building*

*on what you've been given, complementing your basic faith
with good character, spiritual understanding, alert discipline,
passionate patience, reverent wonder, warm friendliness, and
generous love, each dimension fitting into and developing the
others. With these qualities active and growing in your lives,
no grass will grow under your feet, no day will pass without its
reward as you mature in your experience of our Master Jesus.*

When we practice these qualities, hope is alive in the soul. These are
self-disciplines; they shape our behaviors to show genuine Christian love.
Paul suggests similar behaviors that generate hope (Philippians 4:8ff):

*Summing it all up, friends, I'd say you'll do best by filling your
minds and meditating on things true, noble, reputable, authentic,
compelling, gracious – the best, not the worst; the beautiful, not
the ugly; things to praise, not things to curse ... and God, who
makes everything work together will work you into his most
excellent harmonies.*

Paul implies these are aspects of excellence (Paul's word is *arête* – a
Greek ideal, an abstraction). Paul describes the abstract in terms of
behaviors/qualities that generate excellence in the human experience. He
indicates these are natural for the newborn spiritual being.

Paul uses excellence intentionally. He describes behaviors a person
in Christ owns. An initiative is excellent only when it is natural for the person
– by intent and form. The term *arête* doesn't describe what is a **bit** true, or
somewhat noble – it is full, not in part.

Paul's cultural and educational background is in a social context
shaped by mainstream Greek values. Paul was familiar with *arête*, an ethical,
moral and civic standard. Paul finds it valid for the grammar of Christian
experience – a key to understand Spirit-revealed mystery (Col 1:26ff,
Peterson):

*This mystery has been kept in the dark for a long time, but now
it's out in the open. God wanted everyone, not just Jews, to
know this rich and glorious secret inside and out, regardless of*

their background, regardless of their religious standing. The mystery in a nutshell is just this: Christ is in you, so therefore you can look forward to sharing in God's glory. It's that simple.

Christ is in you – don't let this grace go for nothing; use it. Let this energy work in you. In Christ we have a new birth. It is like a new childhood experience ... excellent harmonies, maturing in hope, preparing for our immortal identity.

In 1938, I anticipated Hurffville Grammar School would be "heaven" (which I imagined as real estate). As a Christian senior, I understand "heaven" as an identity – an expected change, a hope. I engage actively with spiritual resources. I prepare for a transition from mortal to immortal. It is a spiritual inspiration Paul shares in I Cor 15:50ff (Peterson):

> *... our natural, earthly lives don't ... lead us ... into the kingdom of God. Their very nature is to die ... but let me tell you something wonderful, a mystery I'll probably never understand ... we are all going to be changed. ... In the resurrection scheme of things, this has to happen: everything perishable [is] replaced by the imperishable, this mortal replaced by the immortal. ... Oh, Death, who's afraid of you now?*

The record of our Judeo-Christian spiritual experience is based on God's engagement with us. Beginning with God's spirit/breath moving through *tohu-wa-bohu* and continuing in the indwelling Holy Spirit. *We are not alone. In life, in death, in life beyond death, God is with us.*

The cosmic expanse hosts glory. We know God visited this small planet as Jesus. Life beyond death is not bound to this time, this gravitational space: Christ is in you, so therefore you can look forward to sharing in God's glory.

Space exploration seeks evidence of water – a life essential. Baptism in water and the Word may be the key to know we are in *Christ*. The re-creating baptism and creating/empowering Word identify this hope:

> *Breathe on me, Breath of God, fill me with life anew,*
> *That I may love what Thou dost love, and do what Thou wouldst do.*

Breathe on me, Breath of God, till I am wholly Thine,
Until this earthly part of me glows with Thy fire divine.

Breathe on me, Breath of God, so shall I never die,
But live with Thee the perfect life of Thine eternity.

Read now the following *Meditation,* which concludes **Exploration III.**

Our culture finds competition exciting: win a game, "top" others,
surpass earlier achievements.
Competition challenges us to identify skills, train and use them.
Human achievement is an accomplishment that is often surpassed.
Mature adults adopt another value: experiencing joyous blessedness.
It's a magnificent God-given gift, not a personal achievement.
Once, I used energy to attain goals as a human being;
now blessedness energizes me as a spiritual being.
Aging may diminish physical vitality and mobility, but the Spirit generates
hope – life energy opening a fine transition to life beyond death.

Blessedness – Discover the State You're In

O the blessedness of freedom from a compulsion to walk among counselors who have no reverence for God, or cluster in shadowy corridors with sinners, or sit among those who scorn righteousness; instead, discover delight in the inspiration and comfort of the Lord's teachings – and value their rightness for every human experience. Such a person is like a tree – in a grove – planted by streams of water: it bears expected fruit, and its leaves do not wither. Every service this person undertakes prospers … The Spirit of the Lord strengthens a righteous person, but the way of the self-content lacks lasting resources. (Psalm 1:1-3,6)

(a personal translation/phrasing from the Hebrew)

Robert Browning's **"Pippa Passes"** celebrates an ideal day!

The year's at the spring
And day's at the morn;
Morning's at seven;
The hillside's dew-pearled;
The lark's on the wing,
The snail's on the thorn;
God's in His heaven –
All's right with the world.

Ah, a blessed moment, a beatitude experience. Hebrew poetry celebrates life as a covenant journey like this. Many psalms are about blessing.

A common Hebrew poetic device compares what is not with what is. Psalm 1 begins with what is not true to covenant rightness – then, affirms it positively.

Verse 1 presents less positive human companions some associate with publicly:

- to <u>walk</u> among counselors who have no reverence for God.
- to <u>stand</u> with sinners in shadowy places.
- to <u>sit</u> with those who scorn righteousness.

We note the psalmist uses specific examples, not generic abstractions: 1) the character of associates; and 2) the relative close associations in successive groups: walk, stand, sit (progressive stages of interpersonal intimacy, all without God, i.e., God-forsaken).

Verse 2 is a doxology; it praises alternative associations, *viz.,* spiritual beings comfortable in a covenant experience. It is not a private quest. It sets covenant blessing in the context of belonging – participation in a spiritual body. The spiritual commitment affects our choices for fellowship, support, inputs, confidants – including partnership with God. What a catalog of benefits:

- delight – all delights satisfy.
- inspiration and comfort – refreshment, renewal, energy.
- the Lord's teachings – covenant is not airy-fairy; the Word indicates both right behavior and points of breakdown.
- values/relevance – our forebears provide testimony of this rightness.

"Delight" is a fruit of rightness shared in the human experience. Good outcomes of the mind, heart, and vitality – our thoughts, feelings, and habitual actions – incrementally magnify worth and purpose.

Verse 3 presents covenant rightness in a nurturing community:

Tree – in a grove: sharing nurturing soil, by streams of water. We have a compound metaphor. Covenant rightness is originally interdependency. Things work together for good because of healthy connections (*... we form one body, and each belongs to all the others.* Rom 5:30-31). Note the inclusiveness indicated in the metaphor:

- tree – indicates individual identity, the significance of self,
- grove – many "selves" in community, covenant needs the body,
- planted – each is rooted in a shared, nurturing environment
    to provide continuity.

The metaphor continues with specific focus: each unit *bears expected fruit – leaves do not wither –* service prospers. Each part values bonding. Note expectations for each unit:

- individual units in the grove generate something.
- creative/redemptive care is inspired (leaves "breathe") –
    brings health.

Verse 6 affirms God's presence in the covenant community – to sustain and redeem. Those who prefer independence and self-reliance seek acreage elsewhere.

Now we return to verse 1. Most are familiar with the translation: *"Blessed is the man/person..."* The phrase *"blessed is"* (in contemporary idiom) generally indicates a cause-and-effect, something occurring in a moment of time. The Hebrew connotes a more expansive and lasting impact: *O the blessedness* ... It puts us in an ongoing awareness and experience, an evergreen life-dimension, a shared benefit – not a tit-for-tat trade-off reaction.

The image draws us outside the privacy of "self" and into covenant community. Its "delight" is a foretaste connected to promised glory – beyond the innate dying aspect of things living in/through time. It is hope. It testifies to God's confirmation/seal for creation: *tov* (Hebrew for "timeless good, rightness"). It is the experience of love celebrated in the currently popular spiritual song Pass It On: ... *once you've experienced it ...!*

I recall festival times in the parsonage as a child – memories about activities in the home and family, e.g., Christmas during the Depression and World War II years. All families had limited resources – but my brother, sisters, and I always had a feeling of abundance! At the end of each Christmas Day, after clearing up the torn wrappings and feasting, all gathered around the tree. By turn, each member in our three-generational family showed and reflected on gifts received. I have a lasting visual imprint of observing my parents during this ritual. Their expression indicated: *O the blessedness!* Few resources, grand rejoicing!

...like a tree in a grove – planted by streams. Many of us "trees" (individuals) transplant ourselves to many "groves" (residences, towns, social contexts) during a lifetime. Hopefully, each move roots us in good soil amid others flourishing by streams enriching body and soul. This provides continuity even in all life's changes.

Shakespeare's tragedies present many heartfelt moments. One cannot miss the intensely poignant pathos of the scene in *Macbeth* (Act V, scene 5) when the king learns his wife no longer lives ... and his spontaneous response from deep within. His inner turmoil rises from his choice of unright action – beginning with the murder of King Duncan. The fruit of his choice is lost *blessedness*, life divorced from the delight of rightness.

Seyton, one of Macbeth's officers and a confidant, returns to Macbeth after learning why women are crying in another chamber:

Macbeth: *Wherefore was that cry?*
Seyton: *The queen, my lord, is dead.*
Macbeth: *She should have died hereafter* [later];
    There [then] *would have been a time for such a word.*
    Tomorrow, and tomorrow, and tomorrow,
    Creeps in this petty pace from day to day,
    To the last syllable of recorded time;
    And all our yesterdays have lighted fools
    The way to dusty death.

Macbeth continues his commentary on his life story as he reflects on it in this moment. It is a *"tale told by an idiot, full of sound and fury, signifying nothing."*

Macbeth, the noble Scot, and his wife make choices – all cast for personal gain by self-serving means. It establishes a chain of actions – each a more devious detour around rightness – like what is described in Psalm 1:1.

A senior's faith seeks an ambience of blessedness. Macbeth found himself far removed from that. Senior Christians seek a blessedness rooted in a right powerfully expressed in Psalm 1:2.

Blessedness is a mark of spiritual maturity, ripeness – nonwithering fruition. We age, yet we are fulfilled: identity, community, continuity. These give faith shape and substance; they validate each self as something more than the sum of its parts. A spiritual being enjoys recurring dawns, each brightened with amazing grace unclouding the mystery of wholeness, holiness. This is the doxology of Psalm 1. Many poets echo the experience through the ages, Robert Browning:

> *God's in his heaven –*
> *All's right with the world.*

Recall Bernard of Clairvaux's hymn captures the psalmist's *delight* of the Lord's inspiration and comfort. It is a delight known to those *in Christ* who near a grander, eternal transition:

> *O hope of every contrite heart, O joy of all the meek,*
> *To those who fall, how kind thou art! How good to those who seek!*

> *But what to those who find? Ah, this nor tongue nor pen can show;*
> *The love of Jesus, what it is, none but his loved ones know.*

Celebrate

The basic meaning of "celebrate" indicates we remember something – we bring it to life, relive the experience. It is intentional; it is how we keep alive value and beauty in who we are, what we are, why we are. Genuine celebration honors interactions and relationships that make up our life story and all its transitions.

"New lives for old!" is a *leitmotiv* (recurring theme) in Jesus' teaching and healing ministry. It is "good news" – but a message not easy to fit into earth experience. After Jesus' resurrection and ascension the message continued. It was done publicly by the Holy Spirit at Pentecost and personalized in Paul's experience on the Damascus Road.

Paul worked through the puzzling features of the experience and articulates it clearly in II Cor 5:15ff (Peterson):

> *...we don't evaluate people by what they have or how they look. We looked at the Messiah that way once and got it all wrong, as you know. We certainly don't look at him that way anymore. Now we look inside, and what we see is that anyone united with the Messiah gets a fresh start, is created new. The old life is gone; a new life burgeons! Look at it!*

Paul establishes a new and bold perspective, and his insights make spiritual experience more specific and valid. This shifts "born again" from the grammar of biology to the grammar of experience. It is the foundation of our identity as spiritual beings bonded in the family of God.

We celebrate this when we gather for worship, especially the Lord's Supper (Holy Communion). Individually and collectively, we honor how God's love benefits us. Broken bread (crucifixion) and shared cup (resurrection) are grace shared with each and all of us. Paul says Jesus ordains these channels of grace (I Cor 11:23-26).

Paul verifies the transition from old life to new life. It is our benefits of God's initiatives (create, redeem, sustain). It reveals a truth: our biological "being" houses a thriving spiritual dimension. Paul's affirmation has fresh impact with Pierre Teilhard de Chardin's insight: We are a spiritual being having a human experience.

Indeed, this makes clearer the ironic twist in the title: *If I Should Die Before I Live!* For seniors, death is not too distant. How magnificent the grace that offers new life now (as continuity with life beyond death)! Indeed, affairs are now soul-size. This gives urgency to what T.S. Eliot calls our "exploration."

> *What we call the beginning is often the end*
> *And to make an end is to make a beginning.*
> *We shall not cease from exploration*
> *And the end of all our exploring*
> *Will be to arrive where we started*
> *And to know the place for the first time.*

For me it was more a redefining awareness than a defining moment. Perhaps a transition more akin to Luke's description of Jesus' "middle years": (Luke 2:52, Peterson): *And Jesus matured, growing up in both body and spirit, blessed by both God and people.*

Surely, I was more aware of self as a spiritual being in September 1960, the onset of an adult exploration. This was not secluded contemplation. This was action – completing prerequisites for a new venture. It was a *hope* moment – very down-to-earth hope for a heavenly inspired, earth-life expectation.

In August, I responded to a beyond-Earth call to Christian ministry. It brought me face-to-face with earthly requirements for professional qualification. The process: steps to attain essential credentials. 1) A denominational credential – church approval as a ministerial candidate. 2) An academic credential – admission to a course of theological studies. 3) An experience credential – intern opportunity.

The presiding bishop approved provisional candidacy for the ministry, pending completion of normal procedures. I began these.

Although late in the season, I applied for admission in an approved seminary program. That was accomplished.

I contacted relevant church officials to seek a "student supply" pastoral assignment. By the end of August, I was assigned a circuit of three small congregations in southern New Jersey's Pine Belt.

With these assurances my focus shifted from expectation to responsibility. The approvals and opportunities brought personal stewardship to the fore. I must perform, meet a standard, be accountable. (I would need – and hopefully get – signs of amazing grace. I must not let this grace go for nothing – II Cor 6:1)

Shortly after Labor Day, I began my first term at seminary. I moved into seminary life and studies easily – earlier doubts quickly fading. Classmates, professors, academic program, campus life blended to make the experience positive, engaging, rewarding generously the investment of time and study.

By mid-September, I was interviewed and formally approved as a candidate for the Methodist ministry. (My father, brother, and brother-in-law were active members of our Annual Conference – the family connection undoubtedly expedited background questions the committee needed.)

My "student supply" assignment began 1 October. The advance "Order of Worship" announced: *"Sermon – Rev. Richard Smyth."* (Gulp! A shock-moment of ice-water reality.) How does a "Rev." know what and how to preach? Casually (!) I brought up the subject with my brother. He suggested I consider the text in Mark 8:34-37. I used the King James' Version I grew up with:

> *Whoever will come after me, let him deny himself, and take up*
> *his cross, and follow me. For whosoever will save his life shall*
> *lose it; but whosoever shall lose his life for my sake and the*
> *gospel's, the same shall save it. For what shall it profit a man,*
> *if he shall gain the whole world, and lose his own soul? Or what*
> *shall a man give in exchange for his soul?*

My academic competence with biblical and theological matters was all of three weeks old! I had few insights – fresh or stale – to shower on people to whom I was a stranger.

So I drew on – was inspired by – the text's litany of strong, challenging verbs as my working framework: *come, deny, take up, follow, save, lost, profit, gain, lose, exchange* (i.e., "get back," redeem).

(During my 50 years of ministry, this text – and these verbs – matured in my understanding and perspective. As I reflect on that first pulpit day, I realize the verb *"follow"* has been prominent for me. I continue to explore its intentions and implications for Christian life.)

The first of three services on my first Sunday began smoothly. The congregation said a Prayer of Confession; I spoke Words of Assurance and led to the Lord's Prayer with these words: *"… the prayer our Lord taught, saying: 'The Lord is my Shepherd, I shall not want.'"* I realized I spoke Psalm

23. The supportive worshippers joined in the beloved Psalm, and we carried on to the Lord's Prayer.

Here I was before a congregation learning my role as shepherd, pastor. My pastoral role involved two days a week. But I had another role – the priority role at this stage. My major obligation as a theological student was spiritual formation. In that my role was a sheep – a learner discovering the dynamics of followership, i.e., representing the Shepherd honestly and honorably.

The roles of shepherd and sheep (indicating guide [*guru*] and follower) are purposeful and heeded ... even with current emphasis on individuality, personal identity, self-sufficiency, level playing fields. Jesus profoundly affirms individual value with the quest to find the "lost." He encourages the found to be in community, to belong. A community models and takes on the character of the leaders it follows.

Jesus describes his shepherd's role with images in John 10. He notes a monitored area of safety, the sheepfold – a place both for individual and shared spiritual development. That's the safe haven for every new creation *in Christ.* Christ, the gate, watches as the sheep discover obedience to service and community. Followership is an inner quality: acceptance and ownership of a moral compass, healthful values, ease with what is right and holy. Its model: the one followed – but never in a mechanical, robotic, or manipulative way.

Jesus, shepherd, no longer leads physically, but we are not desolate. Care comes from belonging *in Christ.* I "hear" Paul celebrating his experience (and I share it) ...*it is no longer I who live, but it is Christ who lives in me. And the life I now live in the flesh I live by faith in the Son of God, who loved me and gave himself for me.* (Gal 2:20) It is a "done deal" – completed, the new reality.

As a senior, I ease myself of "old me" spiritual baggage. The downsizing makes "new me" identity clearer both in earth life and expectation of life beyond death. These resources are sufficient:

- Faith – image God's nature: let benefits of God's redeeming and sustaining initiatives affect my nature.
- Love – I choose behaviors that channel grace for others, I trust. Grace keeps me a good and faithful steward.
- Hope – new life *in Christ* begins to work God's glory in me, even now, and replaces the blankness of death.

These initiatives connect, each melds into the next. They energize continuity. My response to God's re-creating initiatives is acceptance of the gift of new life – self as a spiritual being. This new life impels me to initiate love. Fruits of this love show effects in actions and relationships: ransomed, healed, restored, forgiven ... all marks of re-creation. These keep my senior journey secure *in Christ*. It is stable – even as I deal with ongoing disruptions and distractions. Living as a spiritual being revalues all human involvements. I am grateful for the faith that defines and enriches followership.

I find senior spiritual exploration renews. Involvements are fewer and less demanding, either by choice or by necessity. I confront fewer crises which might compromise rightness. I am free of leadership decision-making but have the opportunity to share expectations. There's more concern for discerning <u>what</u> action is important and right – less with the devising solutions for "hot button" crises. Those still in a more active mode often consult and seek input about <u>why</u> actions are important and effective – not simply efficient.

It's the end-beginning stage of exploration expressed in the Advent hymn "Come, Thou Long-Expected Jesus":

By thine own eternal Spirit rule in all our hearts alone;
By thy all-sufficient merit, raise us to thy glorious throne.

All this keeps my identity clear and content as I enter each new day. It keeps me aware I am a saint – living, not "on hold."

I am down-to-earth, not on a moral high ground. I'm on level ground spiritually, but I consciously honor my steward's calling. Once I was a steward to account for productivity; now it's more quality control of rightness. I sense a personal impact of Gabriel's question to Mary at Jesus' first coming: "*Will you bear God's holiness?*" Will you keep it alive, not just approve or endorse it?

Every saint is a grace-bearer, a medium. The Holy Spirit calls each to bear and witness the holiness; stewards' service is the medium, stewards' faithfulness keeps the message clear. This is seniors' accountability. Ripened maturity knows both means and ends must be right and just.

In the final meditation we considered "blessedness." This invites us to consider the Beatitudes in a senior perspective. (They begin "The Sermon on the Mount," Matthew 5.)

Jesus, the shepherd, faces a congregation pastorally for the first time. He speaks of dynamics in God's kingdom. It's a beginning time; it's an end-time. Jesus offers new guidelines (standards) and opens spiritual exploration to all. For the next three years, Jesus shares the benefits of faith, harvests of love, a hope of life beyond death. But here, in the Beatitudes, he offers blessedness for the journey's complex commitments: *come, deny, take up, follow, save, lose, profit, gain, exchange.*

Seniors' hope rests securely in the benefits of *in Christ* blessedness. The Beatitudes expound on these qualities (Peterson's translation).

You're blessed when you're at the end of your rope. With less of you there is more of God and his rule. God's initiative is faith's firm foundation – in spite of insecurities that unsettle us like an emotional earthquake, wind, and storm. Blessedness is an alternative to do-it-yourself contentment.

You're blessed when you feel you've lost what is most dear to you. Only then can you be embraced by the One most dear to you. Aging often forces radical adaptation: separation from loved ones, friends, cherished conditions and surroundings. Now is the right time to cherish God's presence in holy bonding. It's a special senior call: "Let go and let God."

You're blessed when you're content with just who you are – no more, no less. That's the moment you find yourselves proud owners of everything that can be bought. Let faith make you fully comfortable with your senior-self and learn how to be loving and lovable in your rapidly changing senior community. Fruits of faith and love are not available in retail outlets, eBay, or catalogs!

You're blessed when you've worked up a good appetite for God. He's food and drink in the best meal you'll ever eat. So many adult involvements treat faith and love as either "condiments" to spice up what is bland, or "antacids" for what is too zesty. Blessedness is appropriate "saltiness" – usage that never generates spiritual hypertension.

You're blest when you care. At the moment of being "care-full, you find yourself cared for. Faith-based love is neither intrusive nor self-serving. Intrusive and distorted love comes from self-serving persons who overload gestures with sweetness.

You're blessed when you get your inside world – your mind and heart and strength – put right. Then you can see God in the outside world. Get your followership (your *in Christ* life) in order; that keeps relationships balanced, focused, and relevant.

You're blessed when you can show people how to cooperate instead of compete or fight. That's when you discover who you really are and your place in God's family. So much in life involves competition: seeking influence to claim victories and gain recognition. The good servant's presence never preempts the Master's.

You're blessed when your commitment to God provokes persecution. The persecution drives you even deeper into God's kingdom. (Perhaps Matthew added this in light of opposition from orthodox Jews.) How often, in justice systems (formal, informal), legal process overpowers spiritual rightness. It also reminds seniors to identify a flaw in the *mantra* that urges us to separate sacred and secular perspectives.

The media provide more than enough reports about fragmented morality and questionable ethical commitments. Indeed, did something infect that handful of clay God used, or did some virus get into the life-breath God breathed in us humans? The resounding question: If creation is from God (who embodies rightness), why the clashes and contradictions? Are creation's mechanisms essentially faulty? Are we lost, forgotten?

Alan Paton treats the subject in *Cry, the Beloved Country* (1948). Apartheid divides South Africa by race, greed, limited opportunity, restricted personal liberties. A black pastor's son participates in a group robbery that leads to a white youth's murder (son of the pastor's friend). Two thieves lie to the judge and are freed. The pastor's son tells the truth (at his father's urging); the court convicts him and sentences him to death.

The novel is the basis for a musical drama, *Lost in the Stars* by Kurt Weill. The pastor father's faith is rocked; spiritually adrift, the pastor sings:

Before Lord God made the Sea and the Land
He held all the stars in the palm of his hand
And they ran through his fingers like grains of sand
And one little star fell alone.
So the Lord God hunted through the white night air
For the little dark star on the wind down there
And he stated and promised to take special care
So it wouldn't' get lost again.
Now a man don't mind if the stars grow dim
And the clouds blow over and darken him
So long as the Lord God's watching over him

Keeping track how it all goes on –
But I've been walking through the night, through the day
Till my eyes get weary and my head turns grey
And sometimes it seems maybe God's gone away
Forgetting the promise that we've heard him say
And we're lost out here in the stars –
little stars and big stars blowing through the night -
and we're lost out here in the stars.

The father of the slain white youth seeks and finds the grieving pastor. Both realize a mutual loss: sons – a white son murdered by black attackers, a black son condemned to death by a white man's court. The white father offers friendship to the black pastor. It is accepted. (Grace has a steward.) Reconciliation ... of persons. Redemption ... of hope.

Even in the grievous, complex setting of being "lost," we encounter creation's good is far more lasting than outcomes of human unrightness, sin, and wrong. No citadel of self-sufficiency renders the brooding Spirit/wind powerless. Always that redemptive Spirit comes, serves, offers life.

The opening song of *The Sound of Music* describes the delightful characteristics of Sister Maria. Some sisters mention traits that are not proper behavior for nuns in the Abbey: Maria is tardy, impish, and mischievous, a bit without restraint. Others are charmed by Maria's bright spirit. Still, the question: Is Maria an asset to the Abbey? Mother Abbess notes a special trait: *"How do you hold a moonbeam in your hand?"*

Maria – the moonbeam – captures a Spirit-reality (soul) we cannot measure with mechanisms, manners, and mores. It is a nature that rightly integrates elements of the soul: mind, heart, strength. This is the experience we celebrate as our life *in Christ*. We note changes in how we act.

1) Mind – we look beyond our own "ideas." Over and over we have insights (bits of revelation, perhaps) that are more correct as a way to show love, e.g., Jesus notes the bonding of reconciliation is so superior to separations made rigid by judgments.

2) Heart – determining what is "best" takes us outside ourselves. Any intention for loving action considers the situation and need of the one we seek to help with love.

3) Strength – motivation must consider initiatives – our initiatives – that bring benefits to the receiver, no matter what the sacrifice.

This combination of insight, intention, and initiative specifically illustrate our integrity as stewards, our followership. It draws us again and again to models Jesus revealed in actions and words.

Followership means I own faith commitments and put them into practice. The commitments take various and differing forms as I get older. That is my journey as a saint; I clearly welcome the life-giving Spirit brooding over and in me.

Albert Schweitzer ends his book *The Quest of the Historical Jesus* with these words:

> *He comes to us as one unknown, without a name, as of old, by the lakeside, He came to those men who knew Him not. He speaks to us the same words: "Follow thou me" and sets us to the tasks which He has to fulfill in our time. He commands. And to those who obey Him* [i.e. "hear" Him], *whether they be wise or simple, He will reveal Himself in the toils, the conflicts, the sufferings which they shall pass through in His fellowship, and, as an ineffable mystery, they shall learn in their own experience Who He is.*

Our exploration leads to contentment *in Christ.* Our affairs are soul-size. Our exploration is into God (which Schweitzer expresses in the phrase *"in His fellowship"*). The promise is peace in a mystery made plain, and *"in [our] own experience we know Who [the Lord] is."*

To *"learn in [our] own experience"* indicates activity – never separated from the Shepherd's watchful presence. It implies a right attitude – with grace to keep us at ease as spiritual beings. It implies a covenant faith opening ever-fresh revelation – about God, about ourselves. Often a saint's resources get spoiled or totally exhausted and need support. Even saints are sometimes carried by the Shepherd. Still we journey. John Greenleaf Whittier writes of this in a poem, a familiar hymn:

> *Dear Lord and 'Father of mankind, forgive our foolish ways;*
> *re-clothe us in our rightful mind, in purer lives they service find,*
> *in deeper reverence, praise.*

*Breathe through the heats of our desire thy coolness and thy balm;
let sense be dumb, let flesh retire; speak through the earthquake,
wind, and fire, O still, small voice of calm.*

Paul ends I Corinthians 13 with a glorious invitation for seniors peering anxiously heavenward, considering life beyond death. Paul celebrates: we are not alone. And we have gifts – initiatives of faith, love, and hope. Note vv 12-13 (Peterson's version):

We don't yet see things clearly. We're squinting in a fog, peering through a mist. But it won't be long before the [atmosphere] clears and the sun shines bright! We'll see it all then, see it all as clearly as God sees us, knowing him directly just as he knows us! But for right now, until that completeness, we have three things to do to lead us toward that consummation: trust steadily in God, hope unswervingly, love extravagantly. And the best of the three is love!

We have referred to Paul's insights often in these explorations. And why not? Paul remains a pioneer; he provides a grammar for Christians to express spiritual experience. Let Paul's affirmation cheer us on – Phil 1:6 and Phil 3:14-16 Peterson:

There has never been the slightest doubt in my mind that the God who started this great work in you would keep at it and bring it to a flourishing finish on the very day Christ Jesus appears ... or, our life changes to be in his presence.

And:

I've got my eye on the goal, where God is beckoning us onward – to Jesus. I'm off and running, and I'm not turning back. So let's keep focused on the goal, those of us who want everything God has for us. If any of you have something else in mind, something less than total commitment, God will clear your blurred vision – you'll see it yet! Now that we're on the right track, let's stay on it.

In 1755, John Wesley prepared a service of Covenant Renewal for Methodists to use once a year – traditionally at the beginning of a new calendar year. This covenant commitment can be a seal on our senior's exploration. (Wesley's 18th-century English usage is updated.)

> *O Lord God, I am no longer my own, but yours.*
> *Put me to what you will, rank me with whom you will;*
> *put me do doing, put me to suffering;*
> *let me be employed for you or laid aside for you,*
> *exalted for you or brought low for you;*
> *let me be full, let me be empty;*
> *let me have all things, let me have nothing;*
> *I freely and heartily yield all things to your pleasure and*
> *disposal. And now, O glorious and blessed God, Father, Son,*
> *and Holy Spirit, you are mine, and I am yours. So be it.*
> *And ratify this earth-life covenant in life beyond death.*

Let this covenant establish you as a saint, in that cloud of witnesses. Hold it as a moonbeam to celebrate transitions more serenely.

Truly, this is our certainty as spiritual beings: life *in Christ* has continuity beyond death.

Index of Biblical References

Note: The 1st number indicates chapter; verse numbers follow a colon. Citations may include all or part of verses mentioned. If no verses are indicated the reference is entire chapter.

Old Testament

43:14-19	210
52-53	85
55:3	62
55:11	14
60:1, 3-4, 9	199
61:1-2	50
64:4	80
65:17, 24	80, 147

Jeremiah

| 9:23-24 | 180 |
| 31:33-34 | 58, 128ff, 183 |

Ezekiel

18:30-32	58
36:26-27	128
37:9	100

Amos

| 5:21, 23-24 | 120, 139ff |

Micah

| 6:6-8 | 171ff |
| 6:8 | 131 |

Zechariah

| 4:6 | 181 |

New Testament

Matthew

5	127, 227
5:8	40, 134
5:21ff, 40ff	127
5:48	133
6:22	64
6:25, 33	62
7:7-10	89
7:8	62
7:17	183
8:1-13	145ff
8:21, 22	67
9:9	67
11:28-30	74, 165ff
25:21	31, 184

Mark

1:14-15	37
1:15	19, 21
1:32ff	65

2:32-34	65
4:1-9	37ff
5:11-12	33
8:27ff	104, 115
8:34-37	57, 78, 133, 135, 224
10:13-15	126

Luke

2:29-32	87ff
2:52	223
5:17ff	65
7:22-23	39
7:36-50	151ff
10:25-37	59, 127, 142
11:27-28	126
15:11-32	59, 193
15:17	60
17:20-21	37
19:41	94

Philippians

1:6	231
2:5-11	53
2:12-13	205
3:7-9	90
3:14-15	231
4:1, 7, 11-13	129
4:4, 12-13	164
4:7-9	161ff
4:8, 9	131, 212

Colossians

1:26-27	81, 212ff
1:27	105, 181, 201
1:28	187
3:1	62

Hebrews

12:1	133ff

I Peter

1:3	182
1:13	184

II Peter

1:3, 5-9	211

I John

4:19	127

Revelation

3:20	116, 149
19	210
21	210
21:1-5	199ff, 210
21:3, 5	23
21:5, 6	17

Index of Hymns and Choruses

Index of Authors and Sources

Text of Maori Lord's Prayer *(New Zealand Prayer Book, 1989)*
Eternal Father,
Earth-maker, Pain bearer, Life-giver,
Source of all that is and that shall be,
Father and Mother of us all,
Loving God, in whom is heaven.

The hallowing of your name echo through the universe;
The way of your justice be followed by the peoples of the world;
Your heavenly will be done by all created beings;
Your commonwealth of peace and freedom
Sustain our hope and come on earth.

With the bread we need for today, feed us.
In the hurts we absorb from one another, forgive us.
In times of temptation and test, strengthen us.
From the grip of all that is evil, free us.
For you reign in the glory of the power that is love.

CPSIA information can be obtained
at www.ICGtesting.com
Printed in the USA
BVOW09s2342281117

501521BV00009B/43/P